7 Lessons in NLP

Mo Shapiro

7 Lessons in NLP

Master the Basics of Neuro-Linguistic Programming in 7 Steps

Mo Shapiro

Material previously published in 2020 in *The Ultimate Negotiation Book* and in 2012, 2016 as *NLP In a Week* by Teach Yourself

First published in Great Britain by John Murray Business in 2020
An imprint of John Murray Press

This paperback 2nd edition published in 2026

1

Copyright © Mo Shapiro 2012, 2016, 2020, 2026

The right of Mo Shapiro to be identified as the Author of the Work has been asserted by him in accordance with the Copyright, Designs and Patents Act 1988.

All rights reserved. No part of this publication may be reproduced, stored in a retrieval system, or transmitted, in any form or by any means without the prior written permission of the publisher, nor be otherwise circulated in any form of binding or cover other than that in which it is published and without a similar condition being imposed on the subsequent purchaser.

A CIP catalogue record for this title is available from the British Library

Paperback ISBN 978 1 399 83016 4
ebook ISBN 978 1 399 83017 1

Typeset by KnowledgeWorks Global Ltd.

Printed and bound in Great Britain by Clays Ltd, Elcograf S.p.A.

John Murray Press policy is to use papers that are natural, renewable and recyclable products and made from wood grown in sustainable forests. The logging and manufacturing processes are expected to conform to the environmental regulations of the country of origin.

John Murray Press
Carmelite House
50 Victoria Embankment
London EC4Y 0DZ

John Murray Business
Hachette Book Group
123 South Broad Street
Ste 2750
Philadelphia, PA 19109, USA

www.johnmurraybusiness.com

John Murray Press, part of Hodder & Stoughton Limited
An Hachette UK company

The authorised representative in the EEA is Hachette Ireland, 8 Castlecourt Centre, Dublin 15, D15 XTP3, Ireland (email: info@hbgi.ie)

Contents

Introduction 1

Lesson 1
What is NLP? 2

Lesson 2
Identify empowering and limiting beliefs 16

Lesson 3
Recognize how we and others represent the information around us 30

Lesson 4
Use precision questions to find out what people mean 46

Lesson 5
Identify different communication filters 60

Lesson 6
Use the six levels of change and reframing 74

Lesson 7
Increase your options 90

7 × 7 105
Find out more 111
Answers 112
Further reading 113
About the author 114

Introduction

Welcome to the world of NLP, or neuro-linguistic programming. This book will introduce you to the main themes and ideas that constitute NLP. It will give you an outline knowledge and understanding of the key concepts, together with practical and thought-provoking exercises. NLP has its own language and organizing systems, which are fully explained with examples relating to work and personal issues. The theories and practice of NLP will help you discover what makes some people excel in all aspects of their lives, and will enable you to do the same.

The following lessons provide a dynamic collection of tools, techniques and strategies that can facilitate excellence in all aspects of your life. This book will help you communicate more effectively and develop your interactions by studying:

- the way you access and disseminate information through the language you use
- your perceptions and the values you hold.

NLP was developed to answer the following questions:

- How, specifically, do outstanding individuals consistently achieve the results that make them outstanding?
- What is it that makes the difference between somebody who is merely competent at any given skill and somebody who excels in it?

NLP is based on the idea that mind, body and language interact to create our individual perception of what happens around us and that these perceptions, and their accompanying behaviours, can be changed. Developers of NLP believe that happiness and success are the result of specific patterns of thinking that can be learned by anyone.

Neuro-linguistic programming is something you do already, only you may not *know* you are doing it. Through understanding what works for you and for others, you remove the element of chance and can, by design, create your own effective outcomes in any situation. The better we understand ourselves and others, the better we can change what is not working in our lives and increase what is.

LESSON 1

What is NLP?

NLP, or neuro-linguistic programming, is the study of how human beings make sense of their world. It is a powerful change management tool that transforms the way people think and act. This can have a beneficial impact on users, both professionally and personally.

NLP has been growing in popularity since the mid-1970s. It has many applications in the fields of communication, commerce, personal development and psychotherapy.

Although its early use was primarily in psychotherapy, it was soon clear that NLP had a part to play in the business and commercial worlds. It can be used to relieve stress, improve confidence and tackle problems that people have in their personal and professional lives.

NLP's practical focus on finding what's useful and converting that to action enables teams and individuals to achieve peak performance in areas as diverse as presentations, coaching, motivation, team building, sales and new product development.

In this lesson we will work through the following:

- How NLP developed and its basic features
- The 'principles of excellence'
- The importance of identifying and establishing outcomes.

NLP: thinking, words and behaviour

The way you think affects the internal and external language you use and the concepts you hold. This, in turn, affects the way you behave. We can change our behaviour by changing our thinking and we can change our emotional state by changing our behaviour. It is a dynamic and synergistic process: the whole is greater than the sum of the parts. Any internal or external change to any of the components will have an impact on the whole.

> Neuro-linguistic programming provides a model that enhances understanding of:
>
> ● **Neuro** – your thinking processes; the way you use your senses of sight, hearing, feeling, taste and smell to understand what is happening around you
>
> ● **Linguistic** – your words; the way you use language and how it influences you and those around you. Do your words and the stories you tell put you down or build you up?
>
> ● **Programming** – your behaviour patterns and emotions; how desired habits and attitudes become ingrained and the way you organize your ideas and actions.
>
> NLP enables you to replace negative behaviours and habits with positive ones.

NLP is sometimes referred to as 'software for the brain'. Just as a computer's software defines the way it operates, so your internal programming affects your emotions and the way you behave. If you don't like a particular piece of software, you can change it, in the computer or in yourself.

The history of NLP

NLP was developed by Richard Bandler and John Grinder in the early 1970s as they set out to identify the patterns used by outstanding therapists who achieved excellent results with clients. They discovered a number of processes which they fitted into an accessible model to enhance effective communication, personal change and personal development. They attempted to 'get under the skin' of Virginia Satir, Fritz Perls and Milton Erickson to understand both how they reached their levels of excellence and how to reproduce their skills. Bandler and Grinder wanted to be able to communicate and work with people as effectively as possible. They used their path to discovery as a way of showing others how to achieve success, too. They began to develop NLP by doing it.

Basic operating principles

One of the key drivers at the core of Bandler and Grinder's work was to discover how people excel, especially when managing change. With this information, they devised processes to teach those methods to others.

Their studies indicated that certain basic operating principles, or presuppositions, needed to be in place to create 'the difference that makes the difference'. At first these may seem untenable, even awkward; however, in time they facilitate positive change and can change the way you behave.

Take a few moments to imagine how you might approach situations if you accepted and worked within the 'principles of excellence' listed below. What would it be like if you presupposed these principles to be true? Be curious, and rather than dismissing ideas that don't fit with yours, notice how these principles could strengthen your communications.

> **Basic principles of excellence**
> - We have all the resources we need.
> - The meaning of any communication is the effect it has.
> - There is no failure, only feedback.
> - The map is not the territory: every person's map is unique.

We have all the resources we need

At various points in our life we have achieved success. The findings of NLP suggest that, if we recall the ways we did so, we can transfer these to any present-day challenges. Imagine reaching that longed-for senior position in your place of work. After the initial euphoria, you may wonder what you have let yourself in for. By remembering how you successfully managed changes in the past and re-accessing those resources, you can continue with confidence and anticipate fulfilment. Whether you need confidence, energy, strength or any other personal resource, be assured that you have used it somewhere in your past and can access it again.

The meaning of any communication is the effect it has

> ### Case study
> Colleagues were discussing a fractious decision-making meeting that had just ended. The final decision was made by voting after lengthy discussions to help four 'undecideds' cast their vote and press the 'yes' or 'no' button. 'How did you eventually decide?' Terry asked Sarah. 'I listened to all the arguments and then imagined how they would work in my department.' 'No. *How* did *you* decide?' A confused Sarah answered, speaking slowly: 'I listened to all the arguments and then imagined how they would work in my department.' As Terry was about to ask his question a third time, Ashra translated: 'Which way did you cast your vote?'

What happens when you talk or write to someone and the reply you receive is completely unexpected in content? Sometimes, you will assume that they are being awkward or ignorant in not responding the way you want. As long as you put the onus on them to somehow achieve your interpretation of what is 'right', you cannot change things. However, once you understand your own part in the equation, you can consider doing something different to put across your intended message.

There is no failure, only feedback

How do you react when, in your opinion, things go wrong? Are you a tryer who persists in doing the same thing over and over until, if ever, you get it right? Or do you think it over, and decide what you can do differently for a better result next time?

Think about a time in the past when you know you made a mistake. Imagine calling yourself a failure. What does that look or sound like? How do you feel? Now imagine the same situation and ask yourself 'What could I have done differently to achieve what I wanted? What can I learn?' What does that look or sound like? How do you feel? The notion of learning from feedback means that you are more likely to be flexible than rigid in your dealings with yourself and others.

Remember: if what you're doing isn't working, do something else. Thomas Edison, when called a failure after taking so long to invent the light bulb, responded: 'Every wrong attempt discarded is another step forward.'

The map is not the territory: every person's map is unique

My way of looking at things is unique to me, yours unique to you. If you had chosen to write this book, you may have read all the same research material and taken the same courses as me, yet the end result would have been very different. That is why there are so many reference books available on any given subject.

Think of the people with whom you are in contact at work: internally, colleagues, staff, senior managers; externally, customers and suppliers. How might their 'maps' differ from yours? If you are able to put all the different perceptions together, you will come much closer to a complete picture than if you each stay within the boundaries of your own view. If you accept this NLP principle, then you respect and rejoice in difference.

Choosing outcomes

Identifying and establishing outcomes is a central and first step in NLP. It's easy to say what you don't want. Focusing on an outcome you *do* want creates a much more engaging concept and gives you a clear indication of your commitment. If you don't make the choice for yourself in any aspect of your life, then, by default, someone else will make it for you.

Creating well-formed outcomes

1 Positive
Every time you focus on what you can't do or don't want, you are creating a negative outcome and reminding yourself of what you want to avoid. How would you react if someone said to you: 'Don't look behind you!'? I know I would immediately turn my head. In order to avoid something, I have to think about it, and then react to it. A much more useful instruction would be: 'Keep looking ahead.'

> **Case study**
>
> Divya, a manager in a busy customer-care office, agreed to reduce poor timekeeping in the office as part of her annual appraisal. This was a negative and restrictive outcome. When she decided to put a positive angle on it, she considered the question: 'What do I really want to happen?' She was then able to think about the real issue. Poor timekeeping meant the office was sometimes empty. An empty office led to the 'hotline' phone ringing continuously without being answered, meaning lost customers. What Divya wanted was to maintain existing customers and increase the number of new ones who joined the 'hotline' service. She was now able to think about changing conditions and creating flexible working patterns that would lead to at least one phone being operated all the time – a more creative and outward-looking outcome. She decided to introduce flexible rostering, particularly at 'twilight' and 'sunset' shifts.

2 Specific
Be specific in describing your positive outcome, and use as many questions as you can to check how specific you are. Moving from general to specific enables you to concentrate on answers and solutions.

> Divya asked herself the following:
>
> **Where?** In the red office.
>
> **Who?** I need at least one member of the team to be available for customer calls.
>
> **When?** From 0800 until 2200 hours.
>
> **What?** I will arrange a change of working hours.
>
> **How?** In individual and team discussions and meetings. We will review after the first three months.

3 Evidence

To enhance the energy and application of your outcome, it is useful to imagine as much sensory-based evidence as you can. This will increase your motivation, too. If you do not know when you have achieved your outcome, you could still be using up resources long after you have actually succeeded.

> For Divya, this meant asking: what will I see, hear and feel, and how will others know this has been achieved?
>
> - I'll see at least one phone operator in the room at all times.
> - I'll hear only three rings before the phone is answered.
> - I'll feel confident and relaxed about covering the lines.
>   - They'll be able to see the roster every week, they'll hear words of encouragement from me and they'll feel acknowledged in their needs.

4 Ownership

Whose outcome is it? Be aware of whether you are dependent on someone else for your success. If you are waiting for others to change, you risk becoming a passive spectator. Consider your own part in, and contribution to, the process.

> Divya's key contribution is to identify what she wants, initiate discussion and, having agreed the procedures, to put these into practice.

5 Fit

How does the outcome fit in with other aspects of your life and your overall plan? Are there other people or factors to take into account? If you were to achieve your outcome, how would you feel about it? The response to this last question will indicate how important the outcome is.

> In terms of Divya's 'fit', knowing that customers' calls would be answered and that staff would be clearer about their responsibilities tied in with her being a constructive and collegiate manager. Other areas of the company would be positively affected by additional orders, and they would need to consider the additional administrative impact.

6 Resources

Sometimes, we forget that our resources are internal as well as external. A well-formed outcome will include consideration of both for initial achievement and then continued maintenance. If you accept that you have all the internal resources you need, the skill is to relate them specifically to your outcome. The acquisition of external resources may need greater planning. If you know what you need, you have a much better chance of designing the means of acquiring the requisite resources.

> Divya remembered the time she was on the receiving end of changes at work. She had felt involved and valued when Toby took the time to ask for her ideas and suggestions. She knew she had used his example to create an atmosphere of trust in her team, and felt confident of her ability to listen to their views.

Outcome checklist

Start with the questions below as you create your outcomes. It may be that, as you go through the process, you find you are not meeting all the criteria. Keep amending them until you are happy. This is the linchpin of NLP and will give you the foundations you need for success.

Positive What do you want? What would you like to happen?

Specific Where, who, when, what and how?

Evidence What will you see, hear and feel when it is happening?

Ownership Whose outcome is it, and what is your part in it?

Fit How much do you want it? How does it fit in with other aspects of your life?

Resources Which have you used before that are transferable? Which external resources do you need?

Summary

This lesson has provided an overview of neuro-linguistic programming. As you go through the rest of the book, you will be able to devise your own answers to the question, 'What is NLP?'

We have covered the main principles that underpin NLP thinking, giving you the opportunity to consider those basic presuppositions of excellence that can help you start changing your behaviour and the way you react to yourself, your colleagues, your family and your friends. Although they are not absolute truths, they are useful to stimulate thought, which can help avert misunderstandings.

The section on outcomes is designed to help you clarify and focus on what you want in your life. This will lead to you having far greater chances of success. As you follow the outcome checklist, you can imagine what it would be like if you achieved your outcome and experience it as if it had already happened. This will give you the information that will tell you whether or not this is the outcome that you truly want.

Fact-check (answers at the back)

1. What is NLP?
   a) Software for the brain ❏
   b) A marketing technique ❏
   c) The study of excellence ❏
   d) A change management tool ❏

2. Who co-founded NLP?
   a) Richard Bandler and Paul McKenna ❏
   b) Richard Bandler and John Grinder ❏
   c) Sigmund Freud and Carl Rogers ❏
   d) Carl Jung and Milton Erickson ❏

3. Which therapists inspired the co-founders of NLP?
   a) Fritz Perls ❏
   b) Milton Erickson ❏
   c) Virginia Satir ❏
   d) Sigmund Freud ❏

4. Who can use NLP?
   a) Doctors ❏
   b) Therapists ❏
   d) Anyone ❏
   e) Managers ❏

5. What does the 'N' in NLP refer to?
   a) Neuralgia ❏
   b) Neurosis ❏
   c) Neuro- ❏
   d) Nuclear ❏

6. What does the 'L' refer to?
   a) Logical levels ❏
   b) Linguistic ❏
   c) Language ❏
   d) Legislation ❏

7. What does the 'P' refer to?
   a) Psychotherapy ❏
   b) Principles ❏
   c) Problems ❏
   d) Programming ❏

8. What are NLP principles also known as?
   a) Rules ❏
   b) Beliefs ❏
   c) Presuppositions ❏
   d) Mission statements ❏

9. What do well-formed outcomes need to be?
   a) Realistic ❏
   b) Achievable ❏
   c) Specific ❏
   d) Positive ❏

10. What does NLP offer?
    a) Techniques for change ❏
    b) Strategies for success ❏
    c) Solutions ❏
    d) All of the above ❏

LESSON 2

Identify empowering and limiting beliefs

Have you ever encountered someone who keeps telling you that no one can help them? No matter what you do or say, they will always have a reason why something is not right for them. In the end, you probably give up and thereby successfully reinforce their belief. They are not being deliberately obstructive, even though it may seem that way. They have held their belief for many years and would have to face many challenges in order to let it go.

Such beliefs are so familiar that we often don't know they are there until someone starts to ask questions such as 'Who says so?', 'What would happen if someone *could* help you?' and 'What needs to change for you to be helped?'

In this lesson we will consider the origin of your beliefs, how they influence you and how they can be changed if necessary. We will also think about some additional beliefs that can enhance your communications and behaviour and an NLP technique named 'perceptual positions', which gives you valuable information in understanding another person's perspective.

In NLP it is paramount to start with yourself and understand what drives you to be the way you are before considering other people's styles and preferences.

From beliefs to action

What exactly do we mean when we talk about beliefs? In NLP terms, beliefs represent the assumptions we make about ourselves, about others in the world and about how we expect things to be. These assumptions determine the way we behave and shape our decision-making processes. They are often based on emotions rather than facts. We tend to notice 'facts' that reinforce the beliefs. For example, if you believe that 'everyone is easy to get along with', you will only notice how well you interact with people. If, however, your belief is that 'you can't trust anyone', you will be suspicious and expect to be duped, and the chances are that others will sense this and be wary of you. It's a 'self-fulfilling prophecy': what you believe about yourself is often what happens to you.

Case study

Samir's greatest challenge as a graduate manager was conducting performance reviews with older, more experienced staff. He had been brought up to believe that he should respect his elders and that they knew best. The young Samir took that to mean that he should not contradict or correct older (wiser) people. Stuck with that belief, how could he possibly discuss their underachievement? He knew all about preparation and setting objectives; it was just that every time he thought about one particular staff member, Riannon, he felt increasingly anxious. To make matters worse, she had once mentioned she was old enough to be his mother.

He described what he did at her review: 'I decided to get straight to the point, and indicate where Riannon could make some improvements. Only I seemed to open my mouth and no words came out. She sat there smiling benignly and I told her everything was fine. I couldn't wait for it to be over.'

Samir's underlying belief was limiting his ability to do his job effectively.

Begin to notice which beliefs drive your thoughts, feelings and actions. If your behaviour is not what you want and you think you can't change it, you have probably identified a limiting belief. If your beliefs are supportive and empowering, keep them. If they're restrictive, discard them.

Choices and changes

How do you know what to believe? You don't have to dwell too much on the origin of your beliefs, but knowing from whom or where they came can help you understand what they mean to you. It can also lead you to a way to change. We are generally given injunctions with the best will in the world and for a very good reason at the time. Trace back and identify the roots of what you believe about yourself – notice where your beliefs originate. Can you hear someone telling you to have that belief? Can you picture being told, maybe more than once, or did you just *sense* what was expected of you?

It may well be that you have beliefs that you no longer need, and their purpose is obsolete. If that is so, then change them. Depending on their source, this may seem quite challenging.

> Samir decided to revisit his original belief and work out its meaning and relevance for him now. At school he had always been a quick learner and could outwit his parents in an argument. They felt intimidated, and concerned that his teachers would consider him cheeky. Therefore they wanted him to accept the wisdom of their experience without question – as a protective measure. They also wanted him to progress at school with the teachers on his side.
>
> As you can imagine, this was not the way the young Samir perceived it. Having realized this, now he could start to think it through and consider his choices: either to keep the limiting belief and not question his older staff members, or to find a more suitable and facilitating belief.

> Samir decided that it was important for him to respect other people and himself as equal and different human beings. This was a present-day belief that he knew to be important in all aspects of his life. His feelings about the next review had changed to excited (and a little apprehensive), and he thought about what he would say and how he would say it. He reminded himself that 'There is no failure, only feedback', and he went in search of Riannon to rearrange the meeting, prepared to learn and develop.

Take your time to work through and understand the origin and intention of your beliefs. You can choose whatever you want to believe. Sometimes we choose, or have imposed on us, beliefs that are restrictive in nature. We bring them with us into all kinds of situations. Once we recognize them, we can choose to replace them or discard them completely.

If you approach the question from the other side, you may be following the belief 'I have learned many things in my life. Now is the time to update my repertoire.'

Whether you believe that 'NLP will work for me' or whether you believe 'it won't work for me', the chances are you will be proven right until you investigate the origin of the belief further. Your beliefs can work either with you and for you or despite you and against you. Which would you prefer?

NLP will work for me

- 'I enjoy new ideas.'
- 'I know I can change.'
- 'I've learned so much before – here's another opportunity.'
- 'I've an open mind.'

NLP won't work for me

- 'You can't teach an old dog new tricks.'
- 'I never pick up new ideas.'
- 'I've tried things like this before – they never work.'
- 'Nothing will make me change.'

Which of your beliefs help or hinder you? Compulsive language – which includes the words 'should', 'ought' or 'must' – leads to patterns of behaviour that can become compulsive. If you have a belief that you want to change, you could ask:

- Is this an empowering belief?
- Is this a limiting belief?
- Where has it come from?
- What was the positive intention behind it?
- How do I want to change it?

Which of your beliefs would you like to change? Here's an example:

Belief	Empowering?	Restricting?	Source	Intention	Change
I must not make mistakes	No	Yes	School	Best performance	I can learn from my mistakes

Working beliefs

In Lesson 1, you considered the basic principles of NLP and imagined how it would be if they were yours. These were related to excellence and how it could be achieved. Now we look at the following additional principles, or beliefs, that relate to the workplace.

We come to work to do our best

It is in everybody's interest that their work is as enjoyable and fulfilling as possible. Most people do the best they can, given the system they are in. If you or your company can create conditions in which individuals can take responsibility and feel valued in their role, they will put their best into their job. If someone appears to come to work intent on sabotage, it may be that their needs are not being considered or that their beliefs are contrary to those of the company. They may well be trying to do their best in what is for them a challenging environment.

Our decisions are right at the time we make them

If this is your starting point, you are likely to be calmer and more understanding when you are reviewing performance with your staff. You do not have to accept their decision; just that it was right for them with the knowledge they had at the time. In fact, if you don't accept their decision, then take time to assess whether you have different or additional information that could help them reach another conclusion.

There may even be a chance that, in the light of the ensuing discussion, you reconsider your position. If their decision has resulted in an error from you, remember to think in terms of feedback and learning.

Behind every action is a positive intention

Imagine how it might be if you had this among your working beliefs. It is not always clear why we continue with behaviours that are not apparently beneficial or make no sense to us. What makes us act in a way that sabotages our development? And, if we do so, how does this belief make sense? We need to understand the intention and personal belief behind the action to understand it.

Case study

Ros was a manager who regularly complained of overwork and stayed late most nights to sort out her filing, even though she had clerical assistants in her team. What was her positive intention behind this behaviour?

Ros felt somewhat out of her depth in her existing role. She had always enjoyed general administration and knew this to be an area in which she was highly competent. Her intention, therefore, was to boost her confidence through familiar routine. The effect, though, was to alienate her staff and give herself unnecessary extra work.

There are a number of answers to every question

This is the belief about flexibility and creativity that is central to NLP thinking. If you close your mind to allow in only your own personal beliefs, then you close off many opportunities. If you are working as part of a team and are prepared to listen to all the ideas available, a more satisfactory outcome is likely.

Notice when you switch out of listening to other people's ideas. Does this happen with particular people, subject areas, times or places? Now imagine that these are useful ideas and that you want to incorporate them. This can open up a new way of behaving, thinking and believing.

Imagine that these working beliefs were your own working beliefs, and try them on for a period of time. Notice how they work for you. Write down their effect on you and your colleagues, and where you would like to apply them – for example, in an appraisal, discipline session, selection and recruitment, team meetings or negotiations.

Your colleagues may be surprised if your behaviour changes significantly. Stick with it, and over time you will reap the rewards.

Perceptual positions

One powerful way to increase your effectiveness in relating to others is to extend your information about the way they behave and how they make their choices. The NLP technique called *perceptual positions* provides a practical way to do this. On those occasions when you seem stuck in your communication, it can be very valuable to change your position (literally and figuratively) and take different views of the situation. This is sometimes called *second-guessing*. If you can understand other people's thinking and work out their positive intentions, then you have added knowledge to take you forward.

The three basic perceptual positions

1st position: self – this is your own reality, how you see, hear and feel about a situation. You think and feel in terms of what matters to you.

2nd position: other – this is the other person's reality, how a situation would look, sound and feel if you were them. What might they say or do? How might your input affect them?

3rd position: observer – this is the detached onlooker. How might the situation appear to someone who is not involved? They can watch both parties interact and understand without experiencing either person's emotions.

Within companies, you can become so involved in production or service delivery (first position – *your* map) that you may not know whether your efforts are being channelled in the most productive way. Your many customers will have their own views about your service, and you may find it useful to gain insight into *their* map through the second perceptual position. Ask yourself: 'What would I think about delivery times and quality if I were one of my customers?' The third, observer's, position enables you to assess the interactions between first and second without the emotional interference. You imagine you are *outside* the situation. You could then ask: 'What does the relationship between Shmikes Ltd and its frontline customers seem like?'

Case study

When Hannah was asked to describe her role at work, she said she felt like 'piggy in the middle'. She had the top team complaining about the operatives and the shop stewards expecting her to sort out management.

In **1st position,** she was able to work out what she wanted from the situation – namely, to gain clarity and stand her ground.

From **2nd position**, she studied the other views and beliefs that might be around. She concluded that both the top team and the shop stewards came to her because she was able to communicate equally and fairly. From their positions, Hannah was an objective onlooker who listened to their opinions with no vested interest. The more she considered their positions, the more she was able to see her role as constructive.

In **3rd position**, Hannah noticed that her sense of frustration was blocking her effectiveness and that it would be beneficial if she valued the trust they had in her and could maintain neutrality to help their cause.

Using the three perceptual positions, 'piggy in the middle' became a skilled mediator.

Practise perceptual positions for yourself and notice how they help the situation you choose.

Exercise

- Think of an unsatisfactory situation between you and someone else.
- Put three sheets of paper on the floor, labelled 'self', 'other' and 'observer'.
- Stand on the 'self' sheet, facing the 'other', and recognize how you experience the situation you have chosen. Know how you feel and what you would like to say to the other person. Then move away and turn around.
- Stand on the 'other' sheet and imagine you are that person looking at the 'self'. Recognize how you, as the other person, might experience the interaction. What would you like to say to 'self'? Then move away and turn around.
- Step on to the 'observer' sheet and look at 'self' and 'other'. From this neutral position, notice what is happening. What is or is not being achieved? Remember that you do not take sides: this is the place for objective

> assessment. If you notice any emotions as you stand on 'observer', check whether they belong to 'self' or 'other' and go back to that sheet. 'Observer' is a neutral position. Then move away and turn around.
> - Move back to 'self' and repeat the stages as many times as you need to gain full information and insight.
> - Decide what you will do as a result of your new understanding.

Perceptual positioning is also useful when you are considering launching a new product, have a proposal to make or are checking the 'fit' of an outcome. By thinking in the following terms, you will be able to broaden your approach and increase your flexibility:

- How might other staff feel about this approach?
- How will this look from the customers', suppliers', manufacturers' and employees' points of view?
- What would this sound like to the sales team?

Create some of your own questions to help you collect as many explanations as possible for any situation.

> **'When you already have a belief there's no room for a new one unless you weaken the old belief first.'**
> Richard Bandler and John Grinder

Summary

Now you have been able to clarify those beliefs that are empowering and have started to change or discard those that are limiting. Some of your beliefs, of course, will be easier to change and release than others.

Some of your beliefs are not fully your own, but rather blindly taken on from others. Once a belief is formed, you work overtime to prove it right, even if the belief is something negative such as 'Nobody likes me,' or 'I am a failure'. Consider the following: do you have to let your beliefs govern you, even if they are harmful to others and yourself? Can you consciously make changes to what you believe?

Some of the beliefs you hold give great strength. Studies show that, on average, people who believe they are healthy live seven years longer than those who think they are unhealthy, regardless of their actual health condition at the time of the survey.

Fact-check (answers at the back)

1. What are beliefs?
   a) Assumptions we make about ourselves ❑
   b) Always limiting ❑
   c) Always empowering ❑
   d) Self-fulfilling ❑

2. From where do beliefs emanate?
   a) We are born with them ❑
   b) From our parents and family ❑
   c) From religion ❑
   d) From peer groups ❑

3. Which of these words are associated with NLP beliefs?
   a) Should ❑
   b) Perhaps ❑
   c) Must ❑
   d) Might ❑

4. What characterizes limiting beliefs?
   a) They are unchangeable ❑
   b) They hold you back ❑
   c) They are inconvenient ❑
   d) They have a positive intention ❑

5. What characterizes empowering beliefs?
   a) They make life easy ❑
   b) They can prolong your life ❑
   c) They are good to focus on ❑
   d) They are a gift ❑

6. Which are examples of NLP work-related beliefs?
   a) 'We come to work to do our best.' ❑
   b) 'Our decisions are right at the time we make them.' ❑
   c) 'Our pay is directly related to our skill.' ❑
   d) 'Attitude is more important than qualifications.' ❑

7. How many perceptual positions are there?
   a) Two ❑
   b) Five ❑
   c) Three ❑
   d) One ❑

8. What happens in the third perceptual position?
   a) You incorporate everyone's feelings ❑
   b) You are a neutral observer ❑
   c) You don't take sides ❑
   d) You decide who's right and who's wrong ❑

9. What is the purpose of the perceptual positions exercise?
   a) To test a new product ❑
   b) To understand people better ❑
   c) To change people's mindset ❑
   d) To analyse behaviour ❑

10. What happens in perceptual positions?
    a) You change position literally ❑
    b) You consider your position from different vantage points ❑
    c) You imagine you are someone else ❑
    d) You change position figuratively ❑

LESSON 3

Recognize how we and others represent the information around us

The *neuro-* in NLP refers to the way we use our senses to acquire, process, store and recall information. We use our senses outwardly to perceive the world and inwardly to 're-present' experiences to ourselves. In NLP, the ways we take in, store and code information in our minds are known as *representational systems*.

Memories, for instance, use all the senses. To take one example, a musical trigger might activate memories that lead us to:

- feel the sand
- see the azure sea
- hear the laughter
- taste the food
- smell the spices.

Notice which of your senses are activated when you look at your favourite photos.

Now we will concentrate on the clues and cues that help you recognize your own and other people's preferred thinking and communication styles. In NLP, these are called *accessing cues* because they help you access the way someone is processing whatever is happening around them.

Accessing cues

Eye-accessing cues are probably the part of NLP with which people are most familiar. You may think that all you need to do is watch someone's eyes and then you have all the information you need about them. This is only one part of the story. The knowledge you can gain from observing someone's eye movements relates to their preferred way of thinking about issues. People also give you information through the words they use, the gestures they make and the way they breathe. When you know how someone is processing information, you can work out the best ways to communicate with them.

Representational systems

When someone poses a question or says something to you in a conversation, you may need anything from a fraction of a second to a couple of minutes to process your thoughts and then respond. The way you do this has an important effect on the way you communicate – or miscommunicate – with others. *Representational systems* describe this processing of information.

We represent information internally through our basic senses, i.e. in pictures (*visual*), sounds (*auditory*), feelings (*kinaesthetic*), tastes (*gustatory*) and smells (*olfactory*). The words in brackets are the NLP terminology used to refer to the senses. In general, we all have the capacity to see, hear, feel, smell and taste, unless we have some neurological damage.

> As you **look** at this page in the book, the ringing of the telephone may distract you. As you **hear** your HR manager's voice on the line, you **feel** nervous and slightly apprehensive, wondering about your recent promotion interview. You tell yourself that if you are successful you will go out for a meal at your favourite restaurant. You may remember the last time you ate there, the **smell** of the herbs and spices and the **taste** of the... as you took your first mouthful...

Be aware of how many of your senses you used to follow the above passage. You may have found it easier to picture people or places as you read. You may have been more comfortable recreating sounds or noticing sensations and feelings. The senses of smell and taste may have made you salivate, distracting you even more. What you were doing was using your internal senses to *represent* the external experiences described through the words.

Different people will have different responses. None is right or wrong; they just are. It is important to remember that these comprise information and are not a way of stereotyping or labelling people. The skill is to recognize, without judging, the systems being used and to work with them. Excellent communicators do this instinctively. They move around the *representational systems* to include and reach each member of their audience. In any communication they will use all the three main representational systems (visual, auditory and kinaesthetic) to be sure that everyone can see, hear or make sense of the points they are making. In the same way as our map of the world represents only part of the territory, so our preferred representational system is only part of the picture, or is only one soundbite, or feels incomplete.

Predicates

Predicates are the words we use to distinguish and differentiate between representational systems.

> In visual mode, Sasha would like to **see** the minutes of a meeting written down for her to read. In auditory, Denise would prefer to **hear** what happened or **talk** it over with someone else, particularly the section that wasn't on her **wavelength**. If Phil wanted to **touch** base after the meeting to weigh up his and others' **sense** of the meeting, he would be in kinaesthetic mode. These three could have a frustrating post-meeting discussion if they became stuck in their own preferred system.

Over time, we develop a preference for one of the representational systems, and will tend to use that more often. Although, in different contexts, we will use the other systems, we may often be more comfortable and practised in one of the three. In any discussion where each person is using a different system exclusively, an interpreter may be needed.

Which is your preferred system? Think back to your last meeting or team briefing and record the words to describe it, or draw a diagram. What were the first words that came into your head? Now consider a recent customer meeting, with internal or external customers, and repeat the process. Finally, think about your most recent experience of moving house, and record the words. Did you find your preferred system?

There was probably a strong secondary system and a weaker third. Now listen to and note your colleague's words. When you recognize their preferred systems, you may understand them better. Are you speaking the same language? You may well find that these systems change depending on the context. Notice what happens and extend your knowledge of yourself and others.

Predicate identifier examples

Visual	Auditory	Kinaesthetic	Olfactory/ gustatory
Looks good to me	Sounds right	Feels good	Fresh as a daisy
Outside my picture	Can't hear myself think	Heated debate	Smell a rat
Seeing eye to eye	Singing our tune	On common ground	A sweet person
Shed some light on...	Clear explanation	Hands on	Get the flavour...
Colourful show	Rings bells	Smooth operator	Whiff of success

Eye movements

You can find out more about representational systems via the eye-accessing cues, which concentrate on eye movements. Research in NLP suggests that, in general, people using the visual representational system tend to look upwards or ahead, while those using auditory look sideways and those using kinaesthetic look downwards.

Further refinement indicates that, in general, a right-handed person looks up to their left when they are recalling past experiences and up to their right when they are creating an image, sound or feeling for the first time. For some left-handed people, the patterns are reversed. As this is a generalized model, check your observations in as many ways as you can, using *calibration* as a way of observing each person's unique cues.

As you go through the following exercises, you may find that you respond differently from the suggested eye movements. This does not mean that you are wrong or strangely built; work out your individual patterns.

Visual

A person using visual accessing cues will answer the questions below after locating a picture in their mind. Invite someone to ask you these questions and to note where your eyes go. Then swap with them and note their eye movements. You don't need to speak the answers. What matters is *how* you arrive at them. Analysing eye movements takes practice, and over time you will notice patterns with ease.

> What did your first workspace look like?
> (*Your eyes up and to your left.*)
>
> Imagine your MD with pink hair and wearing a bright orange suit.
> (*Your eyes up and to your right.*)

A person with a preferred visual representational system will want to see diagrams and charts and be more likely to use flip charts or PowerPoint. They may need to see things in writing and prefer email to telephone calls.

Auditory

When people are thinking in sounds, their eyes move across to their left for remembered sounds and to their right for imagined sounds.

> Recite your two times table.
> (*Your eyes across to your left.*)
>
> How would your voice sound under water?
> (*Your eyes across to your right.*)

Those with a preferred auditory representational system will want to discuss issues. They like to talk things over and often 'think out loud' as they gather their thoughts. They tend to prefer the phone to email.

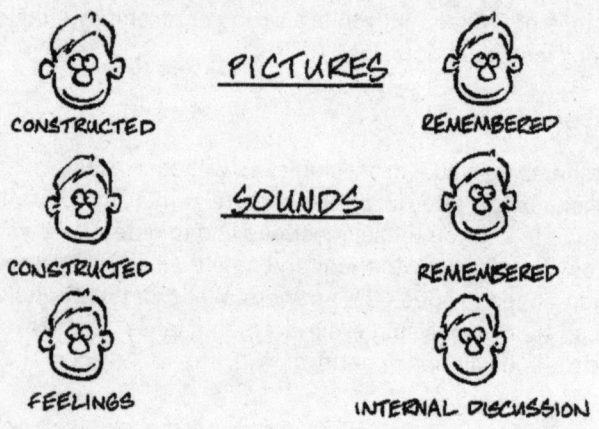

Typical eye-accessing cues for right-handed people as you look at them

Kinaesthetic

If someone's eyes look down and to their right, they are processing in kinaesthetic mode, and this puts them in touch with either their internal emotions or an external tactile feeling. They may also be in olfactory or gustatory mode.

> How do you react when you are angry?
> How would you feel in sinking sand?
> Think of your favourite scent.
> What does ice cream taste like?
>
> (*Your eyes down and to your right.*)

Kinaesthetics will start with their 'gut feelings' in the way they react to different situations. They will want to work out how they feel about an issue – they will often say that they 'just have a sense' about things. They pick up underlying and unspoken feelings.

Internal dialogue

When people are in conversation with themselves – having an 'internal dialogue' – their eyes will tend to look down and to their left. This is another system of thinking, and people can take some time to process their thoughts before they respond. It is often associated with people being 'deep in thought'. The key to communicating with a person using this mode is to give them plenty of time. They can become confused or frustrated if you keep asking supplementary questions through your impatience.

> In quiet times, what do you find yourself thinking about?
> Repeat silently: 'I am who I am and I am fine.'
>
> *(Your eyes down and to your left.)*

QUICK, HIGH PITCH — VISUAL

CLEAR, RESONANT — AUDITORY

DEEP, SLOW — KINAESTHETIC

Please note that these are generalizations. Not everyone fits neatly into them. What you may notice is that, although someone's eyes move in an unexpected direction, they are likely to be consistent so you can learn to recognize their system. Remember to notice their *predicates* (words they use), too, for confirmation.

Body language

The gestures we make, the qualities in our voice and the way we breathe are further indicators of the representational system being used at any time. These may be the first aspects you notice or the final check after you have heard the predicates and detected the eye movements.

Body language and representational systems

	Visual	Auditory	Kinaesthetic
Voice	Speak quickly and in a higher pitch than A or K	Clear, expressive, rich and resonant	Deeper, slower, with pauses
Head	Head up, shoulder muscles tense	Well-balanced or leaning to one side	Angled downwards
Breath	Centred high in chest area and shallow	Evenly over whole chest area	Deep and low in abdomen
Gestures	Exaggerated; sit/stand erect; gestures upwards	Move rhythmically; touching ears or near ears; lips move	Relaxed posture, with rounded shoulders

Calibration

Where eye movements and body language give you a general view of representational systems, calibration involves recognizing and applying the different information that is unique to each person. How is this useful at work? As you become increasingly aware of the individual and minimal cues from a person, you will be able to recognize a pattern from which to assess their mood. You will also be able to evaluate the effect you are having without just relying on the words.

TIP *There are many cues to notice. Some you will already spot subconsciously and just know what someone is going to do or say before they do or say it. Notice the information available from someone's breathing, muscle tone or skin colour.*

Rapport

If your communications always seem to be successful and without conflict, well done. It would seem that you are using all the information available and then adapting your representational style to suit the person with whom you are communicating. This is known in NLP terminology as being *in rapport*.

Rapport enables you to appreciate the other person's map of the world. If you make the effort to be like someone else, they will feel more comfortable in their dealings with you. They are more likely to trust you and do business with you. People tend to like people who are like them. You could also demonstrate rapport by seeing things from someone else's point of view, playing the same tune or getting under their skin in a positive way.

> **'Let me not judge my neighbour until I have walked a mile in his moccasins.'**
>
> Native American proverb

Matching

Rapport is partly established by *matching* the representational systems and body language of others. This might mean sitting down if they are seated, breathing slowly like them or speaking at a fast pace with them. They will have the sense that you are 'with and for' them rather than against them. The advantage of matching is that the other person recognizes at an unconscious level that you understand and value what they are communicating. It will also help you unconsciously to join in genuinely with their understanding.

> **Case study**
>
> Margaret wanted to practise her matching skills. She had been invited to attend a client briefing with a training organization, OT Training, for whom she was the newest associate. She noticed that the client was primarily using an auditory language pattern and sat with his chin cupped in his hands. He also spoke slowly and at an even pace. When Margaret spoke, she matched the rhythm. Whenever he changed his posture, she followed unobtrusively.
>
> She enjoyed the meeting, and was delighted when OT's director rang to tell her that they had gained the contract on the proviso that Margaret was lead trainer.

It is worth noting that you can disagree with someone and still be in rapport: you are disagreeing from as close as you can be to their map of the world. You can also agree wholeheartedly with someone and not be in rapport because you are not 'speaking' the same language. With practice, matching can be performed elegantly and without detection. It is equally important that you match with integrity, not as a cynical means of tricking someone to your advantage.

Mismatching

There may be occasions when you no longer wish to be involved in a discussion or want to switch the focus. Imagine what would happen if you deliberately *mismatched* the other person(s) involved. In most cases, they will respond and move away or change direction. An extreme form of mismatching is turning your back.

Pacing and leading

Pacing extends rapport by respecting and responding to someone's emotional state. When we talk about a person's excitement or enthusiasm being 'infectious', we are merely describing our ability to pace and join in with them. You know what it is like if you go into work full of joy on a Monday morning: if colleagues pace your mood, you continue to feel good. If they say negative things, such as, 'It's all right for some,' or 'Don't know why you're so cheerful. Wait till you see your intray', you may feel deflated.

If you can match and pace someone's mood, then you can *lead* them away from it, too. For example, if someone is becoming increasingly angry at a meeting, you can help them calm down without 'losing face'. Alternatively, in an appraisal meeting, it would be helpful to understand and acknowledge the other person's nerves before creating a more conducive climate. The general rule is to pace a couple of times to make sure you have understood before leading to change. If you start to lead too soon, it will just seem like a mismatch and you will lose the rapport you have built.

Case study

A travel organization wanted to restructure its customer care programme. It called in an NLP expert who introduced a series of ideas including pacing and leading. Staff members were most challenged by irate, often anxious, customers who thought they had been let down by the organization, their main concern being delays and overlong travel times. They practised pacing the 'customer' by matching the energy of the mood and emotions displayed. For example, they talked more quickly, in staccato phrasing and with a sense of urgency.

After a couple of exchanges, they lowered their voice, and slowed their pace and breathing. They had moved to a more resourceful state and started to *lead* to solutions and options. They were overjoyed when their customers followed them and calmed down, too. Both parties had wanted a positive outcome. It was just that they had started from initially incompatible places.

Impact at work

Introducing change in the workplace is more acceptable if you can first match and pace the parties involved. Some basic research about how best to manage information saves time and conflict later on. People like and feel understood by people who are like themselves. So consider: would your colleagues want to see a written account of your proposals, would they rather talk them over, or would they prefer time to grasp and sense the nature of your ideas?

Think how you might approach the situations shown in the table below using each of the three main representational systems. Write or record a prepared statement for each, following the example shown.

	Visual	Auditory	Kinaesthetic
Recruitment interview	We've looked at your CV. Where do you see yourself in five years?	It sounds like you have wide expertise. Tell me about...	In which of your last jobs did you feel most settled?
Closing a meeting			
Staff briefing			
Appraisal			
Customer meeting			

Summary

The way people process information is crucial to communications both at work and elsewhere. When you think about it, it makes perfect sense that conflict can arise when people are processing information in different ways and don't recognize each other's preferences. As you increase your skill in interpreting the mismatches, you will go a long way towards creating more harmonious relationships.

Take your time and focus on the different cues and clues. It doesn't matter whether you start with eye patterns or other people's verbal or body language. You will soon find that you unconsciously understand the representational system being used.

By learning to recognize and understand other people's preferred systems, you can increase your rapport. Notice others who seem to do it naturally. What do they do and what can you learn from them? If there is someone with whom you don't see eye to eye, or with whom you feel out of tune, your challenge is to take your new-found skills, enter their world and change the relationship for the better.

Fact-check (answers at the back)

1. What are the three main senses referred to in NLP representational systems?
   a) Smell ❏
   b) Hearing ❏
   c) Feeling ❏
   d) Sight ❏

2. What do NLP predicates refer to?
   a) Thoughts ❏
   b) Ideas ❏
   c) Words ❏
   d) Phrases ❏

3. Which of these is in visual mode?
   a) Record ❏
   b) Examine ❏
   c) Pressure ❏
   d) Pinpoint ❏

4. Which of these is in auditory mode?
   a) Word for word ❏
   b) Strike a bargain ❏
   c) Make a scene ❏
   d) Hidden message ❏

5. Which of these is in kinaesthetic mode?
   a) Loud and clear ❏
   b) Weighed heavily ❏
   c) Catch a glimpse of ❏
   d) Too much to handle ❏

6. Which representational system is generally indicated by deep, low breathing?
   a) Kinaesthetic ❏
   b) Auditory ❏
   c) Visual ❏
   d) Gustatory ❏

7. What is rapport?
   a) Recognizing a situation you've been in before ❏
   b) Getting along with people ❏
   c) Establishment of trust and harmony ❏
   d) Entering into another person's world ❏

8. What can you match to establish rapport?
   a) Body language ❏
   b) Accents ❏
   c) Breathing ❏
   d) Perfume ❏

9. Why might you pace and lead someone's behaviour?
   a) To increase their energy ❏
   b) To change their emotional state ❏
   c) To gain information ❏
   d) To disguise your feelings ❏

10. What is calibration?
    a) A way of recognizing behaviour patterns ❏
    b) Cues detected through breathing and change in skin colour ❏
    c) A way of regulating behaviour ❏
    d) Something that fine-tunes your communications ❏

LESSON 4

Use precision questions to find out what people mean

In the previous lesson you worked out both someone's preferred way of accessing information and how to establish rapport. However, there may still be areas of misunderstanding. This is because the meaning of the words you use can be more complicated than they sound. You know what you want to say, and you know what the words mean. The challenge arises when you are speaking in your own 'shorthand', expecting the message to be understood, even acted upon, by someone else. It is unfortunate if, as far as the other party is concerned, you have given out only half the 'story', or one that has different interpretations. Words don't always transmit the intended meaning because the audience will interpret them in their own way.

Bandler and Grinder were particularly interested in the patterns of language and behaviour that effective psychotherapists used with their clients to effect change. They observed and modelled the interactions between Satir, Erickson, Perls and their patients that were successful. They concluded that certain types of questions worked and helped people to get better. These questions helped clients to recover 'lost' information, which enabled them to reconnect to their internal experience and so reconfigure their conscious mental processes.

The NLP communication model

The NLP communication model includes the notion that our five senses take in up to 2 million bits of information per second but that our conscious mind can only process 7+/-2 chunks of information at any one time. These can be internal thoughts and feelings or external events and activities.

Obviously there are many things that we do on a daily basis without having to think consciously about them. You weren't aware of the task of reading these words until I just wrote about it and you probably weren't thinking about the texture of the book or the sounds going on around you, until I raised your awareness. And this is as it should be. If we used all our conscious energy thinking about things we do 'naturally' and automatically, then we wouldn't have space to do anything else.

The meta model

Bandler and Grinder developed the NLP process known as the *meta model*. Its aim is to identify the ambiguities in our words and target them with a collection of questions to provide better understanding of the unconscious beliefs, values and decisions they represent. When you want to know clearly and specifically what the words mean, you can use the meta model.

> **Meta model** – a series of devices for achieving a better understanding of vague language patterns, including specific questions for added clarification.

There are times both at and outside work when it is crucial that we are clear and precise in what we say. If you are the health and safety officer who states that, 'There mustn't be too many people at this gathering because of the fire risk', it simply won't do. Equally, if you are talking in terms of a multi-million-pound deal and you suggest a profit share of 'around 10 per-cent-ish', or in an appraisal meeting you say, 'You're always out of touch with the rest of the section', you are not providing information in a form to which others can make a valid response. This is not a case of your being deliberately awkward but simply missing out information that you assume they know. At other times, it may be fine to be imprecise if we are with someone who understands our shorthand or we want to encourage creativity.

Linguistic research suggests that there is a difference between 'deep' and 'surface' structure levels of language. **Deep structure** describes the complete and whole experience you go through subconsciously before saying the words to convey your message. **Surface structure** represents the words you speak both internally to yourself (your own personal shorthand) and audibly to others. It is the conscious representation of your deep structure. If you put all your deep-structure thinking into words, the most basic narrative would take so long that you would lose your audience. Between deep structure and surface structure, we **delete**, **distort** and **generalize** our experience and verbalize the representation.

The meta model provides the techniques to enable you to recover information from another person which they have deleted, distorted or generalized en route from their deep structure. This prevents you wondering if you have guessed right. You can fill in the gaps and reconnect to the fuller meaning. When you are wondering, 'Why are you saying this?', 'What exactly are you trying to tell me?' or 'What do you want me to do?', the meta model provides a set of more elegant questions to help you find out. If we don't ask the questions, we may find we have moved a long way down conflicting paths because of an unnecessary misunderstanding.

Deletions

We delete all kinds of information when we presume that the other person will know what we mean, or when we consider it too trivial to include. Since we can't actively pay attention to everything our senses input, we omit certain parts of our current experience by selectively paying attention to certain other parts of it. That is, we focus on what seems most important at a particular moment and allow the rest to pass us by. The most common deletions occur when people use unspecified nouns, verbs or 'nominalizations', or make comparisons and judgements.

Unspecified nouns

In this pattern, you describe an action without clarifying *who* carried it out. This is sometimes used when the speaker wants to express their dissatisfaction and to avoid conflict by not naming names. It also depersonalizes situations where the speaker seems to be a passive bystander – so taking no responsibility for what is happening.

- 'He's not liked.'
- 'They don't tell you anything.'
- 'It's so difficult.'

- 'Who specifically doesn't like him?'
- 'Who, exactly?'
- 'What, precisely, is so difficult?'

Unspecified verbs

In this pattern, you describe an action without clarifying *how* it was carried out. You may want to understand the behaviour behind a particular action, and you need to know how something was done.

- 'We will be the most efficient...'
- 'She's avoiding me.'

- 'How exactly will we be the most efficient?'
- 'How specifically is she avoiding you?'

Nominalization

'Any *communication* that includes lengthy *discussions* in an *organization* is likely to lead to *confusion*!' What on earth did you take that sentence to mean? It is unclear because it is full of nominalizations.

The word 'nominalization' is used to describe what happens when we take a verb or process which is dynamic and change it into a noun so that it becomes static. (These are also referred to as *abstract nouns*.) Meta-model questions enable us to find out the processes or actions that are missing.

- Any communication
- Lengthy discussions
- Organization
- Confusion

- 'How do you communicate?'
- 'What are you discussing?'
- 'What are you organizing?'
- 'How are you confusing yourself?'

Nominalizations are common in business and politics. They are often deliberately vague and abstract, meaning any number of different things to different people. Nominalizations become a challenge when they are mistaken for reality and we think they actually exist. Nominalizations delete so much information that we take the empty shell and fill it with our own ideas and assumptions. Compare 'raising the stakes' with 'development in investments'. The first describes an active process while the second is static and implies no active participation.

We can recognize a nominalization when the noun makes sense with the word 'ongoing' in front of it. An ongoing relationship or ongoing enterprise will probably relate to an abstract noun, while an ongoing dog won't. The other test is whether or not 'it' will fit into a wheelbarrow. You would struggle to put development or training into a wheelbarrow, whereas several cats, for example, would probably fit quite comfortably.

Comparisons

Sometimes, we can make a statement that implies a comparison but it is not clear what we are comparing. Our listener, rather than assuming that they know what we mean, will want the rest of the information.

- '...resulting in greater customer loyalty.'
- 'She's better at organizing.'

- 'Greater compared to what?'
- 'Better than whom?'

Judgements

> *'It is a truth universally acknowledged, that a single man in possession of a good fortune, must be in want of a wife.'*
>
> Jane Austen, *Pride and Prejudice*

If you heard these ironic opening words of Austen's novel spoken by someone, you might be inclined to reply: 'Says who?' Yet people often make these kinds of global statements, which can be very powerful and often received without question.

The speaker deletes the fact that this is their opinion, and expresses their belief as if it were an absolute fact. They are presenting their map of the world as the only one. In addition, they do not identify who is making the judgement. It may be important for you to know the source of the judgement before deciding on your response. It can also help the other person to consider: 'Who said this in the first instance?' and 'Is it still relevant or useful for me now?'

- 'That is the way to do it.'
- 'His incompetence is worrying.'
- 'According to whom?'
- 'Who thinks he is incompetent?'

Distortions

Distortion is a key component of imagination and a useful tool in motivating yourself toward your goals. When we plan, we use distortion to construct appealing imaginary futures, and we may choose to oversimplify or fantasize about what is possible or what has happened.

Distortions occur when a speaker draws conclusions that have no logical foundation, or assumes faulty connections between different parts of their experience. The skill is to discover what evidence you or the other person has to suggest that their distortion is fact.

Mind reading

These are the kind of interpretations people make when they presume that they know what someone else is thinking or feeling. It is important to check whether this intuitive response to someone is accurate or whether it could be affecting a relationship on the basis of guesswork.

- 'He's ignoring me.'
- 'I'm sure she loves surprises.'
- 'How do you know?'
- 'How can you be sure?'

You can also turn this mind reading around so that you give another person the power to read your mind. They then become responsible for your wellbeing or otherwise, and you can blame them for not understanding you. The classic 'You'd know if you really loved me' is a typical example of this. The meta-model question in response would be: 'What would I know?'

Complex equivalent

This often follows mind reading because it links two statements as if they have the same meaning – for example, 'You are frowning, and that means I'm in trouble.' Here, frowning is equated with being in trouble, which is not necessarily the case: some people frown when they are concentrating. The question for this pattern is: 'How does this mean that?'

- 'He's ignoring me.'
- 'He didn't wave back when I drove past this morning. He must be ignoring me.'
- 'How do you know?'
- 'How does his not waving mean he is ignoring you?'

Cause and effect

This pattern involves one thing having a causal relationship with another. Rather than the complex equivalent assuming that *x* means *y*, here the distortion is that *x* causes *y* and there is some sequence to the events. Use of the word 'but' is sometimes a clue to this pattern.

> - 'I was going to say something but I knew it would ruin things.'
> - 'Involving the top team will lead to solvency.'
> - 'How would saying something ruin things?'
> - 'How will involving the top team cause us to become solvent?'

Presuppositions

These do exactly that and presuppose an underlying assumption about our beliefs and expectations. The classic question 'When did you stop beating your wife?' presupposes that beatings have happened and have now stopped. Whatever your answer, you are in a no-win situation. The responses to presuppositions are likely to include 'What makes you think...?', 'What leads you to believe...?' or 'How do you know...?'

> 'When you go to the meeting, are you voting for or against?' This presupposes that you are going to the meeting and have decided which way to vote. A useful response would be, 'What makes you think I am going? How do you know I'm voting?'

Generalizations

Generalizations involve interpreting one experience as an absolute truth, which applies in all circumstances. They also describe the rules or limits that govern our behaviour.

When these are operating as part of our beliefs, we can seem to be dogmatic and rigid in discussions. Often, there is an element of fear attached to the very idea of being able to change or release these strongly held views.

Universal quantifiers

The language of universal quantifiers is likely to include such words as 'always', 'every', 'never', 'no one', 'everyone', 'all' or 'nothing'. These words are all-inclusive and allow no room for manoeuvre. Using the meta model helps us recognize that our statement is not necessarily based on reality. We can then begin to expand and change our perceptions.

> One response you can make to someone using a universal quantifier is to repeat back the key words with emphasis and then exaggerate to show how inane it is:
>
> 'I'm always the last to know.'
> 'Always? You're right of course. Everyone else in the business world knows before you.'
>
> Take care how you use this or you may not get the outcome you want.
>
> Another response is to check for a counter-argument:
>
> 'Managers don't care about staff.'
> 'Has there been a time when they did?'

Modal operators of necessity

These relate to the conditions and rules by which we run our lives. They implicitly seem to call on an unseen authority or unwritten rules, often originating in childhood. Modal operators of necessity are indicated by words like 'should', 'ought', 'must' and 'have to' or their negative equivalents. These are all words that externalize responsibility. By asking the question 'What would happen if you did not do this?', you elicit the consequences of breaking the potentially constraining rule. This in turn enables the speaker to evaluate the present relevance of this rule.

> - 'I must be available for work.'
> - 'I shouldn't speak to strangers.'
>
> - 'What would happen if you weren't?'
> - 'What would happen if you did?'

Modal operators of possibility/impossibility

When a person says 'I can't' or 'It's impossible', they are talking about something that they perceive to be outside their ability or sphere of influence. In fact, it might just be their perception that is limiting them, not their ability or their situation. If this pattern goes unchecked, it can impair personal development as well as interpersonal relating.

Whenever you find yourself saying 'I can't' or 'I'll never manage that', check whether it is more a case of 'I won't', 'I haven't learned yet' or 'I don't want to.' You can instantly broaden your possibilities. You might also ask yourself: 'What's stopping me?' This will give you many insights into your map of the world.

As with the operators of necessity, you can also ask the question 'What would happen if I did?' This is a very powerful question, and it can empower people to go beyond the barriers they build for themselves.

● 'I can't manage.' ● 'What would happen if you could?'

This statement suggests that the person has some notion of managing – or how else do they know they are *not* doing it? As they consider what would happen if they *could* manage, they imagine possibilities and shift their thinking.

Warning

The meta model can seem either an aggressive technique or overly pedantic. It is essential first to create rapport, so that your questions will be seen as a constructive way of extending your understanding. Take some time to practise the questions in your own way, so that they sound natural.

Summary

The meta model provides an invaluable set of precision questions for when you need or desire to be absolutely clear about what exactly someone is saying to you. Begin to notice any deletions, distortions and generalizations in your own internal dialogue.

Deletion occurs where you omit certain parts of your experience by selectively paying attention to certain other parts of it. By focusing on what seems most important at a particular moment, you allow the rest to pass you by.

Distortion is when you distort your experience of sensory data to make misrepresentations of reality. Distortion may cause you to oversimplify the meaning of events.

Generalization is the process by which you draw global conclusions based on your experiences or other people's rules. At its best, generalization is an efficient means of applying information globally. At its worst, it is taking a single event and turning it into a lifetime of experience.

Fact-check (answers at the back)

1. How many chunks of information does the NLP communication model suggest that the conscious mind can process?
   a) Five ❏
   b) Fifteen ❏
   c) Seven ❏
   d) Ten ❏

2. What is the meta model?
   a) A modelling technique ❏
   b) A set of precision questions ❏
   c) A series of statements ❏
   d) A system that works only with the conscious mind ❏

3. In linguistics, what does *surface structure* represent?
   a) Your complete internal representation as stored in the unconscious mind ❏
   b) The words you speak out loud ❏
   c) The words you speak internally to yourself ❏
   d) The meaning of your words ❏

4. What does transforming deep structure experiences to surface structure communication involve?
   a) Deletion ❏
   b) Creation ❏
   c) Generalization ❏
   d) Distortion ❏

5. Which of the following are examples of deletion?
   a) Mind reading ❏
   b) Modal operators ❏
   c) Unspecified verbs ❏
   d) Judgements ❏

6. Which of the following are examples of distortion?
   a) Mind reading ❏
   b) Cause and effect ❏
   c) Universal quantifiers ❏
   d) Nominalizations ❏

7. Which of the following are examples of generalization?
   a) Mind reading ❏
   b) Presuppositions ❏
   c) Modal operators ❏
   d) Universal quantifiers ❏

8. How can you challenge the deletion 'He's better at managing'?
   a) 'How do you know?' ❏
   b) 'Better than whom?' ❏
   c) 'Better at managing what?' ❏
   d) 'Better than before?' ❏

9. How can you challenge the distortion 'It's bad to be late'?
   a) 'Who says it's bad to be late?' ❏
   b) 'How do you know it's bad?' ❏
   c) 'When were you last late?' ❏
   d) 'When is it good to be late?' ❏

10. How can you challenge the generalization 'She's never on time'?
    a) 'Never?' ❏
    b) 'Not even once?' ❏
    c) 'How else does she let you down?' ❏
    d) 'Have you ever not been on time?' ❏

LESSON 5

Identify different communication filters

At work, do some of your colleagues look forward to the finishing line in a project while others just do not want to be left behind? Do some prefer to check what is wanted through consultation, while others just seem to know what is required and get on with it? Different people in your team will process the information they receive in different ways. Those who operate in the same way as you will seem much easier to motivate, while those who do not may come across as awkward.

The key is to recognize that we each have our own way of filtering and sorting the information around us: none is inherently right or wrong; it is simply the way we do it. In NLP, these filters are called *metaprograms*. When you recognize which filters are being used, you can adjust your communications to fit in with them. Once you recognize someone else's filters, you can work with them from a position of rapport rather than conflict. One of the best ways to motivate others is to recognize and understand how they motivate themselves.

In this lesson you will learn how you respond to information you are given (your filters) and how you programme it. You will also consider other people's filters and how to create rapport with them.

What are metaprograms?

Metaprograms are the internal filters that we use to sort the information we receive in a systematic way, and which then determine our behaviour. They help us deal with the huge amount of sensory-based information in the external environment, organize our thinking and decide where to focus our attention.

If you won a large amount of money tomorrow or were made redundant with a healthy severance package, what changes would it make to your life? Would your answers relate to all the things you could do – sail around the world, set up your own business, write a novel – or to those things you would not need to do any more – stop worrying about bills, not have to go to work, not be cautious when shopping? The way you respond to such questions will give you an idea about the way you filter experiences and information – your metaprograms.

Metaprogram filters

It is important to recognize how flexible people are when they filter or sort their experiences. We all habitually notice some experiences and screen out others, which leads to consistent patterns in the way we think and work.

The reason for identifying someone's metaprogram is to appreciate and understand differences. Once you have recognized the metaprogram, you can work with the person from a position of rapport rather than conflict. The implications at work are immense: rather than being frustrated by someone else's 'pig-headed' disagreements with you, you adapt your interaction to compensate once you identify their metaprogram. You may find you understand them better, too.

Towards/away from

An example of a question to help determine this metaprogram could be the one already quoted: 'If you took voluntary severance tomorrow, what changes would it make to your life?'

Your answer to this question will give you a good indication of whether you move *towards your goals* or *away from unpleasant consequences*. A towards person talks about benefits and knows what they want. An away-from person talks about problems and is more focused on what to avoid than on what to aim for.

At work, a towards person will be a risk taker and will have a 'go for it' approach. They may need an away-from person to anticipate possible pitfalls. An away-from person will put off doing something until the last minute, or until the disadvantages of not doing it become great enough to spur them on. Such a person may also respond better to threats than to rewards. They may need a towards person to give them a push-start.

Sameness/difference

An example of a question to help determine this metaprogram is: 'What is the relationship between the work you are doing now and the work you did last year?'

The answer to this question gives you an indication of whether a person considers information to find similarities and familiarity – 'still looking at' … 'the same as before' – or whether they do so to find difference and exception – 'changed projects', 'new clients with a different slant'. A person who prefers *sameness* will probably be happy to stay in the same or similar type of job and not look for changes. They can often find areas of mutuality. A *difference* person, on the other hand, wants variety at work and is more likely to make a number of career changes. The latter are often the rule breakers.

In addition, there are people whose attention is focused primarily on sameness, with a secondary emphasis on the differences, or people who look for the differences first before considering the similarities. Together, they form a large enough proportion of the population to be the main target for many advertisers. They will reject 'new' unless it is an improved version of the existing model, and will reject 'improved' unless it still has some of the original qualities. What could be better than the familiar with some extra spice?

Internal/external

An example of a question to help determine this metaprogram is: 'How do you know when you have done a good job?'

This is sometimes called the **frame of reference** filter because it refers to the way people make judgements about their actions. An *internally* referenced person would be likely to answer the above question with words like 'I just know' or 'I feel good inside.' On the other hand, the responses 'When someone tells me,' or 'When people use my ideas,' both represent an *externally* referenced person.

Internals are self-motivating people who want to make their own decisions. They work best with minimal supervision, which recognizes their preference to think for themselves. Externals want someone else to set the standards against which to assess themselves. They like to receive clear, positive feedback, and appreciate accessible management.

General/detail

An example of a question to help determine this metaprogram is: 'Tell me about the last film you saw.'

A *general* person would probably give you a broad overview and describe the film as 'a comedy, sci-fi film with excellent special effects', whereas a *detail* person might tell you about the different characters, the subplots, the music and the costumes. A general person thinks about the big picture and overall concepts. They will often leave out the 'small print' and encourage you to 'get to the point'. Their detail counterpart likes to deal with small pieces of data and works well with 'step-by-step' information. They often assess a situation in terms of all the pieces that make up the whole.

Case study

The members of a small amateur dramatics company were all losing patience with one of the actors. She insisted that when the table was laid, the spoons and plates must be in the same place every time, and that someone kept moving

> them. Operating from a detail perspective, she needed to know that the table was set correctly. The director calmed her down by suggesting that the really important thing was to have the correct number of everything on the table, and that the other actors could use their dramatic abilities to move things around.
>
> This seemingly trivial intervention changed a potential lynching into a smoother-running production.

Options/procedures

An example of a question to help determine this metaprogram is: 'Why did you choose your last job?'

Options people would give reasons for their choice such as 'The terms and conditions suited me,' or 'They gave me scope to develop my own style.' A *procedures* person would more likely describe how they chose – for example, 'I bought all the relevant trade journals, selected vacancies in the areas I would move to...' – thus giving you the procedure they followed.

Options people may follow a procedure to begin with and then add variations to suit. They are motivated in a setting where they have freedom of choice to expand the possibilities available to them. The procedures person likes to follow the set task sequence and enjoys doing things to meet the 'standard'. They like a clearly defined course of action and detailed instructions.

Proactive/reactive

An example of a question to help determine this metaprogram is: 'How do you take the initiative?'

Proactive people take the initiative by getting on with things at their own prompting. They are self-starters who shoot first and ask questions later. *Reactive* people wait and respond to others who ask for help. They are good at analysing tasks and gathering information before taking action. Proactive people can make mistakes by ignoring the analysis and planning stages in decision-making. Reactive people may slow things down by too much analysis or because they are waiting for someone else to take responsibility.

Metaprograms in practice

The following table gives an overview of the different metaprograms covered so far. The 'Language' column briefly describes the words associated with each. The 'Work pattern/role' column indicates the areas and types of work that would be suitable for people with those metaprograms. The final column, 'Response', suggests the words you might use to establish rapport with each.

You may want to consider the different combinations and how they work together. You may find you are mainly a towards person who is externally referenced and proactive. Does that suit the job you do? It is worth remembering that your metaprograms are likely to be contextual.

Metaprogram	Language	Work pattern/role	Response
Towards	Get, have, gain, attain, achieve	Sales, innovation	Goal-oriented, incentives
Away from	Avoid, steer clear, exclude, prevent	Problem-solving, auditing health & safety	Point out dangers of not doing
Same	Usual, familiar, always, similar	Mediation, trends, negotiation	In common, traditional
Difference	New, change, one-off, different	Marketing, consultancy	Unique, special, revolutionary
Internal reference	'I decide', 'I made the decision...'	Self-employed, MD	'Only you can decide/will know'
External reference	'What do you think?' 'Is that OK?'	Team player, certificates	'Others think...', 'The facts show...'
General	Overall, big picture, globally	Explorer, policymaker	Basically, framework
Detail	Specifically, precisely	Pilot, architect, finance	Structure, exactly, 'Let's be clear...'
Options	Choice, possibility	Teacher	Brainstorm, variety
Procedure	Necessity, must	Filing, accounts	Known way, proven
Proactive	Initiative, action, future plans	Sales, fundraising, journalist	Independent, direct
Reactive	Respond, reaction, past achievement	Help desk, receptionist	Analysis, waiting

Company metaprograms

It is possible that the company you work in or the managers and staff you work with have similar metaprograms to you. However, if you feel like an outsider, this may suggest that your metaprograms are different in significant ways. It can be very frustrating if you are proactive and your employers are reactive, using crisis management as their norm. Your company may be externally referenced, wanting to know what is going on and what can be learned throughout the industry, rather than just being committed to excellence from within.

Different departments will need people with different metaprograms to be most effective: options people who mismatch will work well in research and development, while detail and procedures people will create an efficient finance section. Teams that have a balance of metaprograms among their members will be more effective.

Sorting categories

Think about your first day at work. The elements you remember will depend on the sorting categories you use. Knowing that none is right or wrong, recognize the way you sort information.

First-day memories might focus on:

- **people** – the person who showed you around, your immediate manager, your team members, new friends
- **places** – the location, your office, the restaurant, the main reception area
- **things** – your desk, chair, computer, paintings, coffee-making facilities
- **activity** – induction, team meeting, staff briefing, phone calls
- **time** – when it happened, dates, what you did hour by hour
- **information** – how you chose the job, why you joined the company.

It is useful to recognize another person's focus of interest in a particular context. Being people-focused is important for staff at the customer interface as they will respond better to the customer's needs. An activity focus will be helpful to someone who is organizing the weekly rotas.

Which focus is important in your job? Which is your favourite sorting category?

Time travel

The way we relate to time also has implications for the way we communicate:

1 Some people seem to live in the past, remembering the way things were. They might talk about how things were done in their last job.
2 Others live for now and their attention is on the present moment. They talk about the here and now and 'Let's do it.'
3 Future-oriented people tend to plan and to be thinking about the future. They are the sort of people who want to know what they will be having for dinner just as they finish their lunch.

Consider which way you and those around you relate to time. What could you change to take you closer to them? There are benefits to any team if you have all three of the above types available, as long as they appreciate each other's value to the team.

Timelines

People code time in different ways. We may use the same words, 'past', 'present', 'future', but we will place them differently in the way we represent them in our minds. How do you know whether something is a past memory or a plan for the future? In NLP, the term *timeline* is used to explain where people position their concepts of time.

Find your timeline

- **Past** Think about four events from your past. Where were those memories positioned? If you were to point to their location, would they be behind you, in front, to the left or to the right of you?

- **Present** As you read this book now, decide where 'now' is. Point to indicate: is it inside you, in front of you, or to the left or right of you?
- **Future** Now think about three probable events from your future, starting with next week and going as far ahead as you wish. Where were those thoughts positioned? Point to their location and notice from which direction they came.

This will give you an idea of where you place time, and if you were to plot and join up the dots, you could trace the direction of your line.

In time

The timeline known as 'in time' is so called because in this representation a person has time passing through them: their past is behind them, their future is ahead of them and their present is inside them. They are *in* their timeline.

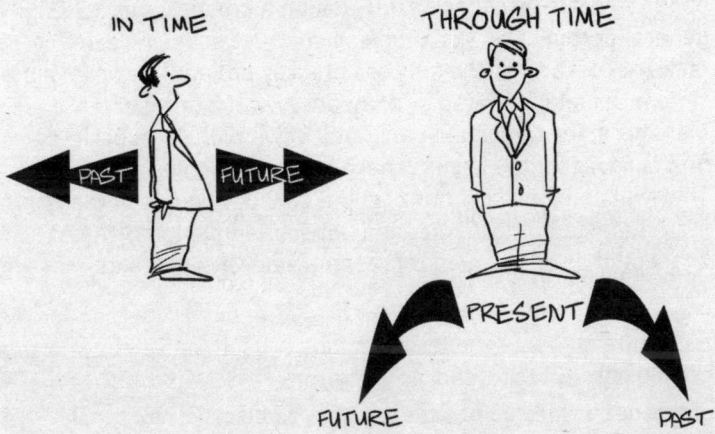

Through-time and in-time timelines

These people tend to concentrate on the present and may be less good at planning and setting deadlines. Their idea of 'urgent' may be quite flexible because they do not strongly connect what they are doing now with what will happen in the future. They can tend to be late because they are so involved in 'now' and easily lose track of time.

Through time

When someone is operating on a 'through time' timeline, they have their past, present and future in front of them. They think of events as a series of related episodes, where time is linear, continuous and uninterrupted. It is likely that through-time people are the designers of time-management schemes, and cannot comprehend how they might be unclear to in-time people. Through-time people tend to arrive on time and place a high value on punctuality. They are also excellent at forward planning.

Chunking

We manage information at different levels and in different-sized *chunks*. You can change the way someone is thinking about an issue by *chunking up* – taking a broader, more general perspective – or *chunking down* – discussing a set of tasks necessary for the success of a key project – or *chunking sideways* – into a related or comparative area of research. Managers need to be able to chunk down high-level projects and purposes into specific, manageable and delegated tasks. They will also have to chunk up the collective goals of their individual staff to form unit and departmental plans. The concept of diversification represents sideways chunking.

Warning

Timelines and metaprograms are generalizations of how people process information and of their resultant behaviour. They are not absolutes, and they will alter with the context. As with all NLP concepts, their purpose is to enable you to think about patterns that help you to understand and communicate better.

Summary

The fact that we all habitually notice some experiences and screen out others leads to consistent patterns in the way we think and behave. In this lesson we have seen how metaprogram filters determine how we unconsciously select what we attend to, which then determines our behaviour. We each have our own way of filtering and sorting the information around us.

Metaprograms are context-specific. The patterns you use may vary in different circumstances: with colleagues, at home, with management and in the family – as a child, parent, sibling or partner. At work you might enjoy taking the initiative and driving things forward, whereas socially you might prefer to react to others' suggestions for an evening out. Nonetheless, you are still likely to have dominant patterns and preferences.

While it is a good idea to resist the temptation to label or stereotype people's metaprograms and resultant behaviour, notice the patterns they regularly use across a wide range of contexts.

Fact-check (answers at the back)

1. What characterizes metaprograms?
   a) They are fixed, not contextual ❏
   b) They help to organize your thinking ❏
   c) They are unconscious filters ❏
   d) They improve your ability to establish rapport ❏

2. What is a 'towards' motivated person?
   a) Someone who puts energy into getting what they want ❏
   b) A risk taker ❏
   c) A person who steers clear of problems ❏
   d) Someone who knows what they don't want ❏

3. What is an 'away from' motivated person?
   a) Someone who anticipates pitfalls ❏
   b) A goal-oriented person ❏
   c) Someone who talks about problems ❏
   d) A person with a 'go for it' attitude ❏

4. What words describe a 'difference' filter?
   a) Familiar ❏
   b) Still looking at ❏
   c) Change ❏
   d) Reorganization ❏

5. What characterizes people with an externally referenced filter?
   a) The need for approval ❏
   b) They are good team players ❏
   c) They prefer minimal supervision ❏
   d) They just know when something has worked well ❏

6. What does the general filter describe?
   a) The small print ❏
   b) The big picture ❏
   c) Broad brush strokes ❏
   d) All the pieces ❏

7. How will a person with a procedures filter behave?
   a) They will stick to the rules ❏
   b) They will describe how they make choices ❏
   c) They will enjoy detailed instructions ❏
   d) They will seek variety ❏

8. What words describe a proactive filter?
   a) Responsive ❏
   b) Self-starter ❏
   c) Wait for instruction ❏
   d) Initiative ❏

9. What characterizes 'in time' people?
   a) They have their past in front of them ❏
   b) They have their past behind them ❏
   c) They concentrate on the present ❏
   d) They tend to be late ❏

10. What characterizes 'through time' people?
    a) They have their present time inside them ❏
    b) They have their present time in front of them ❏
    c) They like to establish deadlines ❏
    d) They consider time as linear ❏

LESSON 6

Use the six levels of change and reframing

We have already considered how our representational systems, language and thinking patterns and filters can explain some of the differences in the way we communicate and process information. Now we will extend that thinking beyond these different perspectives to the different levels of experience that influence the way we live our lives.

We will consider the so-called *neurological levels*, also known as the logical levels of change. Devised by Robert Dilts, this neurological levels model helps individuals and teams align their environment, behaviours, competencies, beliefs and values, identity and purpose, challenging them also to consider a higher purpose – whether work based, family, social or spiritual – in which they make a contribution outside the day-to-day demands of life.

We will also look at the NLP technique of *reframing*, as another way to facilitate change. Reframing enables you to put a new or different frame around an image or experience. What seems to be an extremely challenging situation in the present can be reframed to have less impact when considered as part of your whole life experience.

Neurological levels of change

Robert Dilts, one of NLP's leading thinkers, suggests that there are six levels of learning, communication and change. He terms these *neurological levels* because they fit together in a logical, hierarchical way.

> **The six levels of change**
>
> From the highest to the lowest, the levels are:
> - Connectedness and higher purpose – who else?
> - Identity and mission – who?
> - Beliefs and values – why?
> - Capabilities – how?
> - Behaviour – what?
> - Environment – where and with whom?

Dilts suggests that any changes made at the higher levels will have a greater influence on you than those made at the lower levels. The most important factor for effective change is to recognize the level at which you are stuck in any particular context.

If you have recently been promoted, do you need to change your behaviour to become a more effective manager? Perhaps you still think of yourself as a team member. This is an identity-level issue. Have you ever heard anyone say, 'I can't believe they've promoted me'? This would suggest they are challenged at the belief level and will need to find ways of being convinced that their promotion is totally believable and deserved.

There are some aspects of your life that are so much easier to change than others. One person will think nothing of relocating regularly to progress in their job – an *environmental* change. Another is just as happy to keep changing the job they are doing – a *behavioural* change. A third might want to be a perpetual student collecting qualifications and competencies – a change at the *capabilities* level. Your ability to make these changes easily depends on your beliefs, your identity and the broader systems to which you belong.

Once you can do that for yourself, you will be able to understand and match other people's levels, too. The neurological levels are also relevant to companies.

> ### Case study
> When the directors of Markys introduced an appraisal system across the board, they encountered fierce opposition from their first-line supervisors. This imposed change at the behaviour level did not fit in with the supervisors' views at the identity level. 'We're not managers' was their first response, followed by a capabilities concern: 'We're not trained to do this.' A little research and discussions with the supervisors would have saved Markys from the struggle it went through.

Neurological levels can help you develop greater flexibility in the way you think about all aspects of your life. If you seem to be in an unsatisfactory situation of any kind, you may find that applying neurological-level questions will help you locate and alter the source of your unease. You can use the levels to extend your awareness of what in your life is working for you. The descriptions below explain each neurological level and then offer some applications for individuals and companies.

Connectedness and higher purpose

This level refers to the larger system of which you are a part. In a metaphysical sense, it involves understanding your purpose in whatever you do in the world around you. This is *your* innermost sense of yourself, and it is sometimes called your 'higher purpose'. This level gives you a sense of whether or not you are fulfilled in what you are doing. If your feelings are strong at this level, you may only need to make minor adjustments elsewhere. If this is where you feel unease, then you might need to make changes across the board.

At this level, you would be answering the question: 'Why am I here?'

- **Individual implications:** 'No man is an island', and so whatever changes you make in your life are likely to affect those around you and will include a consideration of your higher purpose. Your decisions about the type of work you would prefer to do will be influenced by the systems to which you want to belong. Given the choice, most people work in settings that complement their ethical position; otherwise they can find themselves at odds with the company mission.
- **Company implications:** companies that attend to their bigger system are concerned about the world in which they do business. To this end, some insurance companies have 'ethical portfolios' which are committed to investing only in projects that make minimal demands on the world's resources.

Identity and mission

Your identity is a description of *who* you think you are, at any given time and in any given role. It is often conveyed in the labels you give yourself. In many cases, these have a qualitative element, for example: 'I am a financial wizard.' As you travel through life, your sense of yourself changes at this identity level and influences some of the options to which you allow yourself to be open. Your identity level can therefore be empowering or restricting of your development. You can enhance someone else's self-esteem by giving them positive feedback at the identity level: 'You are a brilliant organizer.'

At this level you would be answering the question: 'Who am I when I am doing this?'

- **Individual implications:** you will have a number of different identities depending on the context. Think about your identity when you attend a meeting. Are you the chairperson, the minute taker, an expert, a representative, a participant, an observer, an *ex officio* member, a volunteer, or a combination of some of these? When you go to a family gathering, are you a parent, child, brother, sister, aunt, uncle, etc.? The way you describe yourself passes on a message to those around you. It is important that your identity includes a number of different activities.

'It's just the way I am.' 'This is how God intended me to be.' There is often a quite fixed sense of self behind these statements. Some people are frightened that a new identity might fundamentally alter their perception of themselves or others' perceptions. This, of course, ties in with their beliefs, too.

- **Company implications:** the company identity gives employees and customers a clear idea of what to expect from the organization. Where there is a strong figurehead as founder, that person will often incorporate their identities and values into the company.

There is sometimes a challenge when an identity presented to the customer is not applied to staff. 'A company that cares...' may not be consistent in its treatment of its staff. This can percolate through to the way staff treat customers, and the company identity then becomes meaningless. Working with neurological levels can uncover these inconsistencies. There are obvious implications in mergers and takeovers. The new company needs to have a clear identity to share with the amalgamating groups. Staff at all levels can fear being 'taken over' and pushed into an alien identity. If the new identity is discussed and considered as part of the merger package, it can make the transition much smoother.

Beliefs and values

In Lesson 1, we considered the influence of *beliefs* on the way you think, your feelings and how you behave as a result. At the neurological level of beliefs, you are working with what you believe to be true, and this forms the basis for daily action. Some beliefs are handed down through families and go unchallenged from generation to generation. These can take the form of 'sayings', and they are very powerful: 'You can't teach an old dog new tricks', 'If it tastes bad, it's doing you good', 'Learning happens everywhere', 'Life begins at 40.' Can you think of any that are still around for you? Are they helpful or ready to be jettisoned?

Your *values* are the criteria against which you make decisions. They are the attributes that are important to you in the way you live your life. These could include loyalty, liberty and honesty. Your beliefs support and reinforce your values. You have to believe that you can change in order to make changes at any of the neurological levels.

At this level, you would be answering the question: 'Why am I doing this?'

- **Individual implications:** beliefs can promote or inhibit personal growth. Many beliefs are conveyed in thoughts, and they represent your opinion more than firm facts. You tend to notice information that reinforces them and to delete the opposite view.
- **Company implications:** have you ever noticed the passion and zeal in brand-new companies? People here may work exceptionally long hours for relatively little financial gain. The rewards they are getting stem from the firm and shared belief in what they are doing. There is a captivating energy that maintains momentum. As with identity, it is important that the company's beliefs about customers as human beings should also be reflected in the beliefs about staff.

> *'Whether you think you can or whether you think you can't, you're probably right.'*
>
> Henry Ford

There were many limiting beliefs around in the area of new technology. People who for years would have managed their data with a typewriter or secretarial assistance now suddenly found a PC on their desk. The beliefs that might stop them from using the machinery – a PC, a smartphone, a tablet computer or an ebook reader – were based on a lack of confidence or fear of the new: 'I can't work machines', 'It's too complicated, I'll break it' and 'I'm too old to learn.' Contrast these with: 'I thrive on anything new' and 'I can handle it.'

A company's values provide the codes of practice for the workforce, for example equal opportunities and environmental policies. There is obvious discord when the company displays such policies but doesn't believe or practise them.

Capabilities

Your capabilities are the resources that you have available to you as skills and qualities. These may be formally recognized through standards, qualifications and competencies, and will be demonstrated by the strategies you use. Many of your capabilities are processes that you perform regularly, and in many cases they are automatic and habitual.

At this level, you would be answering the question: 'How am I doing this?'

- **Individual implications:** having learned a new set of skills, you might want to consider how you incorporate these. It is great to return from a counselling skills course fired with enthusiasm. If you insist that everyone tells you how they feel all the time, they may react in a negative way. You are only part of the way to absorbing the capability that ensures appropriate use of your counselling skills.
- **Company implications:** companies that want to restructure in some way will succeed if they have considered and attained the necessary capabilities on the way. It may seem a small jump to go from being a photographic studio specializing in portraits to an internet supplier. You will need to know how to create a web page with ecommerce and handle the needs of quite different customers. Your accounting skills and staffing needs will be different, too.

Behaviours

Your behaviours are what you do, what you say and what those around you observe or hear. They are the external representation of your capabilities, beliefs, identity and connectedness. In Lesson 1, you considered outcomes and how to achieve these. One section described being specific. This is very important at the behaviours level. If you have an outcome to aim for, you will be greatly helped by considering the actions you will take to get there.

Behaviours can be easily learned through copying significant *role models* around us. *Modelling* is one of the key NLP skills, and played an important role in NLP's creation. Bandler and

Grinder wanted to know what the key therapists did that made them excellent.

At this level, you would be answering the question: 'What am I doing?'

- **Individual implications:** what do you do to achieve your outcomes, both personal and work-related? You can set yourself behavioural tasks that will enhance your development. You might decide to volunteer to take the minutes at the next team meeting, or to make a tricky phone call that everyone else is avoiding.

    Behaviours are sometimes confused with identity and capability, which can damage a person's confidence and competence. Failing an exam doesn't mean that you are stupid or useless at studying, but, if it is taken at those levels, you are unlikely to seek feedback as to how you can improve. When you are giving or receiving feedback, consider it at the level of *what you do*, not at the identity level – *who you are*. 'You failed this exam but you have passed many other testing situations in your life.'
- **Company implications:** companies behave in many different ways to let the outside world know they exist. They conduct market research surveys and advertising campaigns, they sponsor local charities and send out promotional material to prospective and existing customers. There are set or agreed behaviours that need to be actioned for many company procedures, from allocating petty cash to promotions. These behaviours are lovingly referred to as *red tape*.

Environment

Environment refers to everything that is *outside* you: where you are, the people you are with, your home, your work – your surroundings.

At this level, you would be answering the questions 'Where?' and 'With whom?'

- **Individual implications:** your choice of where to live will be influenced by your identity. If you have to move, you would also consider environmental-level factors such as schools,

public transport, green space, distance from friends, etc. Where you go and what you do socially can all be considered at the environment level.
- **Company implications:** the comfort and safety of your surroundings make a big difference to how well you work and how satisfied you are. Considerations at this level could include who you lunch with, how you are as a co-worker and your effectiveness in an open- or closed-plan office. Many people will tolerate a poor working environment if they have good relationships with their work colleagues.

Describing change

The following sample table illustrates how someone may describe their desire for change. Read the words and note the implications: these give you a broad idea of which levels would benefit from change. In the table, a nurse is describing his dissatisfaction with work at each level. The questions in italics are ones that might facilitate his change.

In this example, you could help the nurse at any of the neurological levels. The six levels are interactive and influence each other. Changes at one level will effect change at the levels below, but changes on the lower levels will not automatically cause change at the higher levels. If he were to change and believe he was good enough, he would acknowledge that his skills were valid, he would behave differently and he would be able to move on in the way he needed.

Neurological level	I don't enjoy nursing any more.
Purpose	I don't know why I am doing this any more.
	What were your reasons for becoming a nurse?
Identity	I don't like the person I become when I'm nursing.
	Who do you want to be when you are nursing? How might you become a person you do like?
Belief	I don't believe I'm good enough any more.
	How were you good enough in the past? What would make you believe you are good enough now?

Neurological level	I don't enjoy nursing any more.
Capability	I need to update my training.
	How could you do that? How do other qualifications and experience count?
Behaviour	I don't have enough time to do all I need to.
	What do you have enough time for? What do you do well?
Environment	It might just be this area.
	Is it this specialism, this ward or this hospital? What are the hospitals like in other areas?

Think about an issue that is not right for you at present. In which level is it based? Where might you start to intervene? Once you start to ask yourself the right questions, you may find you move around the levels. How much change or development do you want? Take time to notice whether you have certain levels at which you prefer to operate – how do these compare with colleagues'? If you work in a team where there is friction, it may be that each team member has different ideas at the values or beliefs levels, and that these need to be addressed.

Reframing

In NLP terms, a *frame* is the focus of attention you give to something. If you look at a picture from one side, it may appear quite different than from another perspective. The value of reframing is in being able to consider an issue from many different angles. If you have ever put a picture or photograph into a new frame, you will know how much that can alter it. That is what you can do with behaviours or thoughts that seem stuck.

Reframing is a way of getting people to say: 'How else can I do or consider this?'

Context reframing

Context reframing enables you to recognize that there is a positive place for almost any behaviour – doing the right thing in the right place at the right time. Embarrassment is sometimes the result of just getting the time or place wrong. Next time you find yourself or someone else limiting themselves with phrases like 'I'm too sensitive, too careless, too slow', or 'I wish I could stop doing...', use reframe questions to find a context in which the behaviour is appropriate and positive:

> **Question:** 'When would it be beneficial to be sensitive?'
> **Answer:** 'When I notice someone in the office who is nervous or unsure.'
> **Question:** 'Where would being slow be an advantage?'
> **Answer:** 'In a meeting that is making decisions about budgets.'

Content reframing

Content reframing is where you change the meaning of a seemingly limiting behaviour. You might want to use content reframing next time you hear statements like 'My mind goes blank when I stand up to make a presentation,' or 'I get upset when I make mistakes.' Your aim is to find another, more useful meaning.

> **Question:** 'What else could going blank mean?'
> **Answer:** 'It could mean I'm clearing my mind to concentrate on what I want to say.'
> **Question:** 'What is the value of getting upset?'
> **Answer:** 'It shows how much pride I take in doing a job well.'

Remember that, in Lesson 2, Hannah used perceptual positions to reframe her description of her role at work. She changed from the frustration of being 'piggy in the middle' to become a more acceptable skilled mediator.

Checklist for change

The following table gives you an idea of the questions that will help you to check which level or levels are problematical and how to address the issues they reveal. Where things are already going well, you can use the levels as a guide to making your situation even better as they extend your awareness of what in your life is working for you.

Neurological level	Meaning
Connectedness and higher purpose	Why you are who you are. What you are here for. How you can be fulfilled. Is there more involved than the obvious? Your contribution to society.
Identity	Who you are – i.e. what role(s) do you play in this context? What is your identity relative to those around you?
Beliefs and values	Your values, what you believe. Your expectations about this situation. What is important to you.
Capabilities	What you can do. What are your skills? How are they relevant? How do you apply them?
Behaviour	What you do and how you behave.
Environment	Where you live, work and play. The physical, social and emotional environment.

Summary

This lesson focused on *change*. With the neurological levels model, you were able to understand how the different levels of thinking interact. The model gives you a framework with which to organize and gather information in order to identify the best point for intervention and to make or suggest changes. The levels can help you develop greater flexibility in the way you think about all aspects of your life.

In addition, we considered the technique of reframing challenges, limiting thoughts and behaviours, working from the premise that 'choice is better than no choice'. For example, the arrival of rain is joyful in a drought-ridden environment and most unwanted on a camping trip, outdoor wedding or much-awaited barbecue. It is all a matter of which frame you use.

Fact-check (answers at the back)

1. Which of these are NLP's models and techniques for change?
   a) Representational systems ❏
   b) Reframing ❏
   c) Seeing life as a journey ❏
   d) Rapport ❏

2. In the neurological levels hierarchy, which levels are below the identity level?
   a) Capabilities ❏
   b) Higher purpose ❏
   c) Environment ❏
   d) Beliefs and values ❏

3. What would you ask at the level of higher purpose?
   a) How does this contribute to the greater good? ❏
   b) Why am I here? ❏
   c) Who else may be involved? ❏
   d) Whose fault is it? ❏

4. What would you ask at the level of identity?
   a) Why me? ❏
   b) Who am I? ❏
   c) What roles do I have? ❏
   d) What kind of organization are we? ❏

5. What would you ask at the level of beliefs and values?
   a) Why am I doing this? ❏
   b) How do I know what to believe? ❏
   c) What is important to us? ❏
   d) How do I affect others? ❏

6. What would you ask at the level of capabilities?
   a) What do I need to do here? ❏
   b) Who can help me do this? ❏
   c) What skills do I have? ❏
   d) How am I doing this? ❏

7. What would you ask at the level of behaviour?
   a) What am I doing? ❏
   b) How could I do this better? ❏
   c) How does this behaviour limit me? ❏
   d) How can I change your behaviour? ❏

8. What would you ask at the level of environment?
   a) What are the external influences on me? ❏
   b) Where does this happen? ❏
   c) Who is involved? ❏
   d) How does this affect global warming? ❏

9. How can context reframing be described?
   a) Almost all behaviours are useful or appropriate in some context ❏
   b) Doing the right thing in the right place at the right time ❏
   c) Changing the location of a seemingly limited behaviour ❏
   d) Providing a focus for your thoughts and actions ❏

10. What does content reframing mean?
    a) Changing the meaning of a seemingly limited behaviour ❏
    b) Having more resources through having more perspectives ❏
    c) Having a major influence on how you interpret and react to your experiences ❏
    d) The meaning of a situation is determined by what you choose to focus on ❏

LESSON 7

Increase your options

Wouldn't it be good if you could change the way you approach and react to a variety of different situations, instead of feeling there is nothing you can do about them and telling yourself, 'That is just the way things are'? One way to increase your options is to give more attention to what works in your life rather than being stuck with what doesn't work. If you have been successful, confident and motivated in any aspects of your life, you can use those experiences to be so again in many situations. This is another opportunity to use the presupposition, 'We have all the resources we need,' and act as if it were true.

In this lesson we look at three techniques to enhance your flexibility before outlining where you might go next:

1 Submodalities can help change the way you code your memories. You cannot change what happened, but you can change the way it affects you now.

2 Anchors are naturally occurring stimulus–response connections. You can create your own anchors to trigger a particular state or emotion in a specific future context.

3 Modelling is based on the NLP presupposition, 'If one person can do something, anyone can learn to do it.' You will have the chance to observe and recreate someone else's successful behaviours or attitudes.

Submodalities

In Lesson 3 we considered representational systems and how these are an expression of the way we think and process information. Within each of these systems we can now make finer distinctions, which give us more data about the quality of our experiences. These distinctions – called *submodalities* in NLP – describe how we refine our sensory experiences. They are the foundation stones of the senses, characterizing how each picture, sound and feeling is composed.

> **Submodalities** – how we code experiences and distinguish different sensory systems.

If you're thinking *visually*, the pictures in your mind's eye will, for example, include colour, movement, shape or dimension. Thinking in *auditory* could have sounds – melody, rhythm or tonality. *Kinaesthetic* thinking could include temperature, texture, weight or location.

Submodalities make the difference between an experience you remember as positive and one that you would rather forget or that makes you cringe when you recall it. Once you recognize your preferred method of coding, you can choose whether or not to change the code. This is particularly useful when you want to replace an unmotivated state with a more motivated one, or to lessen the impact of a painful past event. Some people tend to store their memories in a way that leads to negative, low-energy reactions, or to anticipate future events with worry and anxiety. By changing their submodalities, they can alter their whole experience.

What is different about those days when you just can't seem to get out of bed and those when you're up bright and early, raring to go? Some people see the day ahead as dark and cold, and all they can hear is a morbid drone. On the other hand, on their good days, everything is brighter, they feel full of energy and they enjoy listening to the birds singing sweetly. Once you recognize the words that describe your 'good' days, you can choose how to use them.

Find your preferred submodalities

1 Think about a task that you don't like. As you do so, notice whether you recall pictures of the task, the words or sounds associated with it or the accompanying feelings.

- Write down or record a description of what came into your mind, and be as detailed as you can.
- Stop thinking about that experience, move around and think of something else.

2 This time, think about a task you really enjoy and take on with vigour. As you do so, notice whether you recall pictures of the task, the words or sounds associated with it or the accompanying feelings.

- Write down or record a description of what came into your mind, and be as detailed as you can.
- Stop thinking about that experience, move around and come back to now.

3 Compare the lists and notice what kind of words you have used to describe your motivated and unmotivated states.

Which submodalities are the difference that makes the difference?

What you have now is an indication of the way your thinking about a situation can make it pleasurable or not. If you accept that a memory is simply that – an event that happened and cannot be changed – why spend time wallowing in the bad moments and letting them influence the way you run your life? By changing your submodalities, you can change the impact and meaning of your thoughts. You can also change your approach to any outstanding tasks. Your submodality distinctions may have been visual, auditory or kinaesthetic.

Visual

- in colour, black and white or shaded
- brightness: dull or shiny
- clarity: dim and hazy, or sharp and in focus

- size: larger than life, life-size or smaller
- framed or panoramic
- location: in front, to one side or behind you
- clarity: blurred or in focus
- associated, i.e. seen through your own eyes, *or*
- dissociated, i.e. watching yourself in the picture.

Auditory

- volume: loud or quiet
- words or sounds
- stereo or mono
- distance: close or from afar
- tone: soft or harsh, and whose voice(s)?
- speed: faster or slower than usual.

Kinaesthetic

- pressure: hard, soft or a sense of being pushed
- texture: rough or smooth
- weight: light or heavy
- location: where in your body do you experience sensations?
- shape: angular or curved
- intensity: strong or weak
- temperature: hot or cold.

Change your submodalities

1 Go back to a task that was not one of your favourites.

2 As you think about it this time, consciously make it bigger, brighter, more colourful and closer to you. Imagine yourself doing it rather than looking on from the outside. Use a positive tone of voice to tell yourself how good it will be when you have done it. Imagine feeling satisfied, with a great sense of achievement.

3 Play around with your submodalities and notice the way they change the impact on you.

You can make changes in any situation. If you don't like the result, change the submodalities back or try something different.

There are some general trends in the submodalities connected with feeling confident and motivated. Pictures here tend to be associated, big and bright. Sounds are clear and normal pace. Feelings will be solid and warm. The way we talk about our inner thoughts also reflects our mood, and thus 'I always look on the bright side', for example, is preferable to 'The future looks black.'

Next time you are thinking about a painful or unpleasant memory, make the picture dark, small and far away from you. Change the voices to comic ones like Donald Duck's, and change the music to honky-tonk. Then notice the difference in the way you relate to it.

Anchors

In NLP terms an anchor is any stimulus which evokes a consistent response. This can be practical (e.g. the sound of a fire alarm, which means 'Stop what you are doing and move outside') or emotional (e.g. a photograph of a loved one, which makes you feel happy and valued). The power of anchors is based on our ability to learn by making links and forming associations. Once established, they become automatic responses that can be beneficial or detrimental to you. The *beneficial* anchors are those that trigger resourceful states such as confidence, energy and creativity. The *detrimental* anchors activate unresourceful states such as depression, frustration and lethargy.

> **The power of anchors**
>
> You've had a stressful day at work. You get into your car or on to the bus or train and listen to your 'soothing' music or take a favourite route home. This will calm you down, possibly slow you down and alter your stressed state into a more congenial one. On the other hand, you could get into your car, bus or train, and go over in fine detail all the elements of the meeting that stressed you. You might sit down with a thud, grip the steering wheel tightly, or clutch your briefcase and newspaper tightly and glare at anyone who considers sitting near you. This will keep you fired up and speeded up. I wouldn't want to be the next person to meet you!

By choosing affirmative anchors, you can calm yourself down and ensure that the stress is left behind where it belongs and you can carry on more positively with the next part of your day.

What works for you?

If you are nervous or apprehensive about making a presentation or team briefing (or anything you still have to do), you can now choose resourceful anchors to change your approach. The good news is that if you accept the NLP operating principle that we've discussed – 'We have all the resources we need' – then you can transfer what you do well and resourcefully from one part of your life to any other part of your life that you choose. You may feel highly creative when decorating your home, and now you can take that creativity into presentations, report writing or negotiations.

Think of a situation at work or outside where you would like to be more resourceful. Then decide which resource(s) you need to become so (e.g. confidence, calmness, energy, concentration or humour).

Locate the resource

Think about a time in the past when you have fully experienced that state you wish to draw upon. It doesn't matter how long ago it was or whether it was in your professional or personal life. Relive the experience now, seeing the people and things around you as you did at the time. Hear the sounds again, the voices, other noises or maybe the silence. Savour the positive feelings that accompany the experience. Make sure that you are fully associated into the experience, not an onlooker. As you recall the resourceful time, you may also notice physiological changes that indicate a sense of wellbeing. Enjoy this intense feeling of being in your chosen state.

Choose your anchor(s)

You may prefer a *visual* anchor like a particular scene, person or object. An *auditory* anchor would include sounds, music or voices, and a *kinaesthetic* anchor could involve a gesture to recreate the emotions, sensations and feelings. To create a very powerful trigger, you may choose to have all three available. You may see a riverside scene, hear the word 'relax' and squeeze your fingers together to switch yourself instantly into a relaxed state. Do you have a lucky outfit or interview suit? These are anchoring you kinaesthetically because you feel confident and comfortable in them. They are also visual anchors because you like the way you look in them. If they are very bright, they could also be 'loud' auditory anchors!

Decide what your anchor will look, sound or feel like. Make it different from your regular behaviour so that you don't confuse it with other states and resources. Also, choose something discreet that no one else will notice.

Put them together

Return to the resourceful time in the past. Re-experience it again and connect with being there. When the feeling is strong and reaching its peak, implement your anchors. See the picture, hear the sound and feel the gesture. Hold them for a few moments and then release them. Then shake yourself or move in some way to bring yourself back to the present.

Test it

Remember the initial situation in which you wanted to be more resourceful? Think about it now and, as you do so, fire your anchors when they will be most useful as you go through the situation. How did you react? Has your thinking about the original situation changed? Notice that you can now switch to a more resourceful state instantly.

Anchoring is a skill that needs practice. It becomes easier and more effective the more you use it. The more you use it, the more it will become part of your unconscious behaviour. Notice those that already work for you and aim to use them more. Notice also how you anchor 'unresourceful' states such as bad moods and debilitating anxiety. Change the anchors and observe what happens. With resource anchoring, you can increase your emotional choices.

Modelling

As we noted previously, NLP itself was conceived by working out how excellent therapists communicated with their clients. Bandler and Grinder did not 'become' Satir, Erickson or Perls; they learned how to think like them, *modelled* them and then applied that thinking to NLP.

> **Modelling** – the process of understanding the thoughts and actions of successful people that enable someone to accomplish a task excellently.

Children learn much of their early behaviour through modelling the people around them. It is not surprising that many will share any key interests or hobbies that their parents enjoy. There is a saying, 'Imitation is the sincerest form of flattery', and people do indeed want to be like the people they admire. NLP is not suggesting you can become someone else, just that, if you can understand what makes them achieve so much, you can model it yourself and then apply your learning to increase your effectiveness.

Great achievers, particularly in sport, will often claim that they modelled themselves on a childhood hero in the same field. They watched how they perfected their game, noticed how they walked or ran, and imagined how it would be when they were like their hero.

The modelling process

There are three parts to the full NLP modelling process:

1 **Using the second of the perceptual positions.** This involves studying the behaviours of the person you want to model and understanding as nearly as possible their map of the world.

Ask the question: 'What would I have to do to think and behave like you – as if I were you?'

2 **Testing the model.** Do this by taking out one element at a time as you use it. Notice the effect: does its removal make any difference? If 'no', you don't need it. If 'yes', then you have identified an essential element.

3 **Designing a way to teach the skill to others.** This has clear implications in an organizational setting. You can study the excellent staff in any section and, through coaching and mentoring, pass on the relevant strategies to enhance the skills of the relevant personnel.

Modelling exercise: key questions

1 Identify the skill you want to model and reproduce. (You can model yourself and transfer an effective strategy of your own into different settings.)

2 Select a person or people who demonstrate excellence in this skill.

3 Observe and identify:
- their behaviour – what they do and how they do it
- their representational systems and body language
- their filters and metaprograms
- their neurological levels.

4 Where possible, it is useful to interview your model to obtain a clear understanding of what they do. Don't be surprised if they are not clear: they will probably do a lot of it unconsciously. If, for example, you wanted to know how someone successfully negotiated a pay rise, ask:
- 'What do you think about before you go to see your manager?'
- 'How do you help yourself feel confident?'
- 'What sorts of questions do you prepare, and how many do you have?'
- 'How would you describe yourself in the situation?'
- 'How do you prepare to compromise?'

Next steps

This section has given you the basic tools for understanding neuro-linguistic programming and an overview of some of the main themes and thinking that make up NLP. It is a vast area of study and people are finding new applications all the time. Although the techniques and models are derived from a combination of NLP thinkers, by definition, they represent *my* map of the NLP territory. Follow up the bits that have most interested you and enjoy where they take you. Practise establishing rapport in your communications and understanding which representational systems are being used. Use the submodalities to change your responses to past events and, along with anchoring, to positively prepare for the future.

With NLP, you can increase your choices about how you feel and react in any situation and extend your repertoire in communications with others. It is up to you where you go next.

You may want to go back and assimilate the ideas you have read about, or experiment further with the exercises. Please change any of them so that they make best sense for you. You might decide that you would like to take a course or study further.

Know your outcome

If you have some ideas about your future with NLP, this is also an opportunity to revisit the questions related to outcomes. What do you want to do with NLP? Is it something you think will help with family, friends, at work or purely to enhance your own development?

Be flexible

Flexibility is a key element of NLP, as you will have realized. It encourages you to be open to options in the way you behave and communicate. Try out lots of different behaviours and techniques to find out the kind of responses you get. Notice the way other people are thinking and the words they use. Practise the exercises with friends or colleagues. Some may take longer than others to comprehend fully. Start with those that first caught your eye, sounded good or just felt right.

Instead of staying stuck in any situation that isn't working for you, repeat the following sentence:

> ***'If what I'm doing isn't working, I'll try something, anything else.'***

Summary

A key aim of NLP is to help you move from situations you don't like or that aren't working for you to ones that are. In this lesson we've examined three ways of increasing your ability to make positive changes.

Using submodalities, we learned that we can keep our pleasant thoughts and memories uppermost and dynamic in our mind and move our unwanted thoughts and memories far away into some distant, less central place.

We all create and respond to positive and negative anchors, but once we recognize them and their effect on us, we can keep or change them. What are your significant anchors? For example, what pictures form the background on your computer or phone? Make sure you choose anchors that make you feel good, happy, relaxed and confident.

Modelling suggests that we can learn how a successful person achieves their success. They become our model. Replicating a particular behaviour involves more than just imitating that behaviour. It involves releasing our limiting beliefs and identifying the values and beliefs that drive their behaviour and the specific skills that enable those behaviours to happen – the 'why and how' of something a person does well.

Fact-check (answers at the back)

1. What do the submodalities do?
   a) Give you more information about the quality of your experiences ❏
   b) Help you differentiate between 'good' days and 'bad' days ❏
   c) Describe your unconscious thoughts ❏
   d) Relate to representational systems ❏

2. What do submodality distinctions in visual mode include?
   a) Volume ❏
   b) Weight ❏
   c) Clarity ❏
   d) Size ❏

3. What do submodality distinctions in auditory mode include?
   a) Volume ❏
   b) Rhythm ❏
   c) Clarity ❏
   d) Intensity ❏

4. What do submodality distinctions in kinaesthetic mode include?
   a) Volume ❏
   b) Temperature ❏
   c) Clarity ❏
   d) Texture ❏

5. What generally happens when we feel confident?
   a) Pictures are associated and bright ❏
   b) Sounds are muffled ❏
   c) Feelings are cool ❏
   d) Inner thoughts are of a bright future ❏

6. What characterizes anchors?
   a) They keep you stuck in one place ❏
   b) They are automatic responses ❏
   c) They occur naturally ❏
   d) They are different in different situations ❏

7. What is the purpose of establishing an anchor?
   a) To trigger a particular state or emotion ❏
   b) To make you a better communicator ❏
   c) To access a particular state or emotion ❏
   d) To change other people's behaviour ❏

8. Why does NLP use modelling?
   a) To enable you to become someone else ❏
   b) To increase your behavioural repertoire ❏
   c) To understand someone else's behaviour ❏
   d) To model human excellence ❏

9. When modelling, what can you observe and identify?
   a) Behaviour ❏
   b) Emails ❏
   c) Body language ❏
   d) Musical preferences ❏

10. How can you improve your NLP skills?
    a) Television programmes ❏
    b) Workshops ❏
    c) DVDs ❏
    d) One-to-one coaching ❏

7 × 7

1 Seven key themes

- **Know what you want (goal setting):** Well-formed outcomes are an important tool for ensuring that you get more of what you want in your life.
- **Know whether you're getting what you want (sensory acuity):** Once you know where you want to go, you need to be able to notice – using one or more senses – whether or not you are going there. Sensory acuity trains our minds to see and listen to non-verbal communication.
- **Get the attention of the unconscious mind (rapport):** Rapport – the process of building and sustaining a relationship of mutual trust, harmony and understanding – happens when two people's behaviours match.
- **Adjust what you're doing accordingly (behavioural flexibility):** When you notice that you are not getting what you want, or when what you're currently doing isn't working, you need the flexibility to change what you are doing in order to get a different result.
- **Model excellence:** A NLP presupposition is that 'if one person can do something, anyone can learn to do it' (within physical, practical and psychological limits). With that person as our model, all we have to do is release our own limiting beliefs, work out how they do the thing we want to do and start to apply their methodology.
- **Identify limiting beliefs:** Often based on emotions rather than facts, beliefs are the assumptions we make about ourselves and others and about how we expect things to be. These assumptions determine the way we behave and shape our decision-making processes. We tend to notice 'facts' that reinforce the beliefs. It is almost as if we attract only ideas that feed rather than contradict our beliefs.
- **Use the bell jar distraction technique:** Imagine you have an inverted bell jar surrounding you. This container acts as

a barrier and stops other people's negative thoughts and feelings from reaching or touching you. Let the past go and forgive. Dragging your past with you only slows you down.

2 Seven assumptions to live by

- **The meaning of your communication is the result you get.** In other words, it's up to you to get others to understand your message. You have to take responsibility for your communication.
- **We are all unique.** Every human being – even an identical twin – has their own unique way of understanding and interpreting the world. We all think differently.
- **There is no such thing as failure – only feedback.** Information you receive about something you did is simply that, information or feedback. It's about your actions and has nothing to do with you personally.
- **Behaviour speaks louder than words.** Listen to what people say, but pay more attention to what they do. If there is any contradiction between the two, look for behavioural evidence of change and don't just rely on people's words.
- **We cannot not communicate.** As long as you are awake, you are communicating things about yourself without using words, simply by the way you stand or sit or even breathe.
- **You have within you all the resources to achieve what you want.** Most of us can do most things that we want. Sometimes we just need to be reminded how to do it.
- **Behind every behaviour there is always a positive intention.** Whatever a person's behaviour may be, they have a positive purpose for behaving in that way.

3 Seven great quotes

- 'Keep your thoughts positive because your thoughts become your words. Keep your words positive because your words become your behaviour. Keep your behaviour positive because your behaviour becomes your habits. Keep your habits positive because your habits become your values.

Keep your values positive because your values become your destiny.' Mahatma Gandhi

- 'I've learned that people will forget what you said, people will forget what you did, but people will never forget how you made them feel.' Maya Angelou
- 'You can conquer almost any fear if you will only make up your mind to do so. For remember, fear doesn't exist anywhere except in the mind.' Dale Carnegie
- 'If you don't make decisions about how you are going to live in years to come, then you have already made a decision – to be directed by environments instead of shaping your own destiny.' Anthony Robbins
- 'I never hit a shot, not even in practice, without having a very sharp, in-focus picture of it in my head ... the final scene shows me making the kind of swing that will turn the previous images into reality.' Jack Nicklaus
- 'Nothing can stop the man with the right mental attitude from achieving his goal; nothing on earth can help the man with the wrong mental attitude.' Thomas Jefferson
- 'The best thing you can do is the right thing. The next best thing you can do is the wrong thing. The worst thing you can do is nothing.' Theodore Roosevelt

4 Seven tips for using NLP

- **Anchor great emotional states** in people, such as: learning is easy; a curious state of mind; enjoyment; contentment and so on.
- **Use stories and metaphors** to change content, context and meaning. The unconscious mind loves to hear stories. They're a powerful form of change.
- **Be flexible:** remember to use your immense flexibility to get your desired outcome. If what you're doing isn't working, do something different.
- **Always be in rapport** with the other person when using NLP.

- **Use perceptual positioning** to work out what's going on between you and another person. You can't really understand someone until you 'walk a mile in their shoes'.
- **Reframe to accept or change behaviour.** Behaviours are rarely wrong in themselves: they just occur in the wrong context.
- **Focus on what works.** NLP asserts that the conscious brain carries a maximum of nine pieces of information at any one time.

5 Seven principles from NLP

- NLP has four pillars on which to build success: know what you want; understand others and let them know you understand; be prepared to change what you're doing and your goals; experience the world and process information, using all your senses. Use these pillars to support you to be open to previously unexpected possibilities.
- Your mind is your internal powerhouse that steers your thoughts and subsequent actions. The messages and thoughts from your mind influence the way you feel and the actions you take.
- It's not what people say to you that affects you but what you say to yourself afterwards that makes the difference. NLP recognizes the impact our language has on our lives. Use language that helps and inspires you.
- You always have a choice, though you may not seem to. NLP suggests you find at least three ways of doing something.
- Change your physiology to change your state. If you're feeling stuck, angry, unhappy or unmotivated, do one or more of the following to change your mood: walk around; dance to some jazzy music; jump up and down; relax; sing out loud.
- Mental rehearsal – also known as visualization – is practice in the imagination, which prepares and primes the body for an actual situation. Use it to help you run through what you want in your mind before experiencing the actual event.

- Recognize your own and other people's motivation direction. A 'towards' person will be a risk-taker and have a 'go for it' approach. They may need an 'away' person to anticipate possible pitfalls. An 'away' person will put off doing something until the last minute, or until the disadvantages of not doing it become great enough to spur them on. 'Towards' people respond better to rewards, 'away from' people to threats.

6 Seven great coaching questions

- **What do you want?** This is the ultimate NLP coaching question. Many people only know what they don't want. Once you help someone state their goals in positive terms, you can both work out the steps needed to get there.
- **What would happen if you did?** When a person says, 'I can't' or 'It's impossible', they are talking about something that they perceive to be outside their ability or sphere of influence. In fact, it might be just their perception that is limiting them, not their ability or their situation.
- **What's the best question I could ask you now?** Rather than scrambling around to ask the 'right' question, trust the other person to know what is best for them.
- **How do you stop yourself?** It takes a lot of energy for someone to keep a problem in place. This question subtly suggests that they are the one with the power to move it.
- **Always?** Generalizations involve taking one experience and making it an absolute truth in all circumstances. They also describe the rules or limits governing our behaviour. These words are all-inclusive and allow no room for manoeuvre. This question is designed to identify and challenge the thinking.
- **Where, when and with whom (do you want)?** It's important to put goals into context and describe a goal in as much detail as possible, for both the conscious and the unconscious mind of the person.

- **If you did know, what would be the answer?** This is a great question to use when people say, 'I don't know.' It's imperative to be in rapport with them, otherwise the question can seem glib and provoke a defensive response.

7 Seven influential people

- **Richard Bandler:** Bandler, the co-founder of NLP, has changed therapy, education and medicine for ever. His record of helping patients deemed incurable is unsurpassed.
- **John Grinder:** The co-founder of NLP, Grinder has devoted his life's work to his quest to uncover and present human patterns of excellence, modelled from geniuses in different fields. He created NLP with Bandler as a means to investigate and replicate human excellence.
- **Milton Erickson:** Erickson believed the unconscious mind was self-generating, positive, and key to successful change. The purpose of therapy is to access unconscious resources.
- **Virginia Satir:** Satir was one of the pioneers of family therapy, and a major source of NLP patterns and distinctions.
- **Shelle Rose Charvet:** Known in the NLP community as the 'Queen of LAB Profile' (Language and Behaviour Profile), Charvet developed an in-depth insight into metaprograms.
- **Anthony Robbins:** One of the foremost authorities on the psychology of peak performance, Robbins is the guru of personal, professional and organizational turnaround.
- **Sue Knight:** Knight is the author of *NLP at Work*, the book that pioneered the application of NLP to business.

Find out more

If this book has whetted your appetite and you want to take it further, there are many resources for you to do so. You can learn from one-day taster courses, weekend workshops or NLP practitioner courses. Check that your trainers are accredited and have trainer or master trainer qualifications. Take time checking that their way of thinking and training works for you.

Read some of the other authors listed at the end of the book to broaden your map. Watch DVDs or YouTube clips, listen to CDs or take a training course. To find training courses and practitioners, visit:

- Association of NLP – www.anlp.org
- International NLP Trainers Association – www.inlpta.co.uk
- The Professional Guild of NLP – www.professionalguildofnlp.com

Whatever you do next... enjoy getting to know yourself and making sense of what makes you the unique person you are.

Answers

Lesson 1: 1b & d; 2b; 3a, b & c; 4d; 5c; 6b; 7d; 8b & c; 9c & d; 10d.

Lesson 2: 1a & d; 2b; 3a & c; 4b & d; 5c; 6a & b; 7c; 8b & c; 9b; 10b, c & d.

Lesson 3: 1b, c & d; 2c & d; 3a & d; 4a; 5b & d; 6a; 7c & d; 8a & c; 9b; 10a & b.

Lesson 4: 1a & c; 2b; 3b & c; 4a, c & d; 5c & d; 6a & b; 7c & d; 8b & c; 9a & b; 10a & b.

Lesson 5: 1b & c; 2a & b; 3a & c; 4c & d; 5a & b; 6b & c; 7b & c; 8b & d; 9b; 10b & d.

Lesson 6: 1b, c & d; 2a, c & d; 3a & c; 4b, c & d; 5a & c; 6c & d; 7a, b & c; 8a, b & c; 9a & b; 10a, b & c.

Lesson 7: 1b & d; 2c & d; 3a & b; 4b & d; 5a & d; 6b & c; 7a & c; 8b, c & d; 9a & c; 10b, c & d.

Further reading

Alder, H., *NLP for Managers: How to Achieve Excellence at Work* (Piatkus, 1996)
Andreas, S. & Andreas, C., *Change Your Mind and Keep the Change* (Real People Press, 1988)
Bandler, R., *Using Your Brain – for a Change* (Real People Press, 1997)
Bandler, R. and Grinder, J., *Frogs into Princes* (Eden Grove, 1990)
Bavister, S. and Vickers, A., *Essential NLP* (Hodder Education, 2010)
Charvet, S., *Words That Change Minds: Mastering the Language of Influence* (Kendall/Hunt Publishing, 2010)
Knight, S., *NLP at Work: The Difference that Makes a Difference in Business* (Nicholas Brealey Publishing, 2002)
McDermott, I. and Jago, W., *The NLP Coach* (Piatkus, 2002)
McDermott, I. and O'Connor, J., *Practical NLP for Managers* (Gower, 1997)
Molden, D., *Managing with the Power of NLP for Competitive Advantage* (Pitman Publishing, 1997)
Molden, D., *NLP Business Masterclass*, 2nd edn. (Financial Times/Prentice Hall, 2007)
O'Connor, J. and Seymour, J., *Introducing NLP*, 2nd edn. (Thorsons, 2003)
Overdurf, J. and Silverthorn, J., *Training Trances* (Metamorphous Press, 1995)
Quilliam, S., *What Makes People Tick?* (Element Press, 2003)
Robbins, A., *Unlimited Power* (Simon and Schuster, 2001)
Shapiro, M., *Shift Your Thinking, Change Your Life* (Sheldon Press, 2001)
Shapiro, M., *Presenting: Bullet Guide* (Hodder Education, 2011)
Steinhouse, R., *How to Coach with NLP* (Pearson Education, 2010)

About the author

Mo Shapiro, partner of INFORM Training & Communication, is a Master Practitioner in NLP and Coaching. She has an outstanding record as a communications and presentation skills coach and trainer and as an international public speaker. Mo contributes regularly to all broadcast media, has also authored *Interviewing People Successfully in a Week*, and co-authored *Tackling Tough Interview Questions in a Week* and *Job Interviews in a Week*.

RAISING READERS
Books Build Bright Futures

Dear Reader,

We'd love your attention for one more page to tell you about the crisis in children's reading, and what we can all do.

Studies have shown that reading for fun is the **single biggest predictor of a child's future life chances** – more than family circumstance, parents' educational background or income. It improves academic results, mental health, wealth, communication skills, ambition and happiness.[1]

The number of children reading for fun is in rapid decline. Young people have a lot of competition for their time. In 2024, 1 in 10 children and young people in the UK aged 5 to 18 did not own a single book at home.[2]

Hachette works extensively with schools, libraries and literacy charities, but here are some ways we can all raise more readers:

- Reading to children for just 10 minutes a day makes a difference
- Don't give up if children aren't regular readers – there will be books for them!
- Visit bookshops and libraries to get recommendations
- Encourage them to listen to audiobooks
- Support school libraries
- Give books as gifts

There's a lot more information about how to encourage children to read on our website: **www.RaisingReaders.co.uk**

Thank you for reading.

hachette UK

---

[1] OECD, '21st-Century Readers: Developing Literacy Skills in a Digital World', 2021, https://www.oecd.org/en/publications/21st-century-readers_a83d84cb-en.html

[2] National Literacy Trust, 'Book Ownership in 2024', November 2024, https://literacytrust.org.uk/research-services/research-reports/book-ownership-in-2024